Praise For Stepping Out Of Eden

Over the centuries, there have been many different theories about which essential qualities and characteristics can be understood to be uniquely human. In *Stepping Out Of Eden*, Dr. Rita Louise explores an impressive body of comparative perspectives on the subject, drawn from many different fields of study. These range from archaeology and anthropology, psychology and behaviorism, to ancient mythology, spiritualism, shamanism, ritual, and religion. A comprehensive, informative and enjoyable read!

– Laird Scranton, author of *The Science of the Dogon*

Stepping Out Of Eden, raises questions many of us have but few of us ask. Where do we come from? How did we arrive at our present state of evolution? Is there a purpose behind it all? Where are we headed? What comes next? In this wide-ranging, cross-disciplined montage, Dr. Rita Louise takes us behind oral histories, religious texts, and archaeological mysteries, to confront essential unknowns and ask important questions about our very existence as a species. Strap yourself in for quite a ride!

– Jim Willis, author of *Ancient Gods: Lost Histories*

Stepping Out Of Eden presents a deep investigation of what the author calls the mythic narrative. And in doing so she exposes a trove of ideas from across a wide spectrum from fields of study which easily helps the reader to find a firm understanding of who we are.

Unafraid to tackle controversial theories Dr.Rita Louise ushers in with firm intellect and experience to demonstrate a systematic break down process explaining just how complex we are as a species. And I would add that after reading this book, how ambiguous our world and our ancient history continue to remain. But no longer are they so elusive that we find ourselves hindered in our efforts to continue seeking answers; and especially with the help of Dr. Rita's new book.It helps! From ancient medicine, rituals to myths, she manages to present well written and brilliant ideas revealing a structured and fun methodof thought. This is a book I strongly recommend.

–Anthony F. Sanchez, author of *UFO Highway*

In her integrative *tour de force* of our *homo sapiens* species on our home planet Earth, author, naturopathic physician, medical intuitive, and psychic healer Dr. Rita Louise lovingly guides our intuition to an scientifically informed Inner Standing of how we humans are designed from inside outto manifest inside our Universe of time, energy, space and matter withinthe interactive dimensional ecology of a humongous Multiverse as Souls based in the Spiritual dimensions of the Omniverse

– Alfred Lambremont Webre, JD, MEd, author of *Omniverse*

Dr. Rita Louise has an uncanny ability to not only swamp us with fascinating facts about our ancestry, but leaves us in a state of amazement at the depth and complexity of her research. Whatever we may have thought of our ancient history, Dr. Louise will turn it upside down, substantiate her conclusions with an abundance of facts from diverse sources. All this to solve the mystery of what it is to be human.

A new mystery unfolds on every page. The book reads like a detective story which leads us to most surprising conclusions. Don't miss it. It will amaze you, but most of all; it will leave you greatly surprised.

– Stanislaw Kapuscinski, author of *Delusions*

STEPPING OUT OF EDEN

Rita Louise, PhD

Copyright © 2018 by Rita Louise, PhD

No part of this book may be reproduced or utilized in any form or by any means: electronic, mechanical or otherwise, including photocopying, recording or by any informational storage and retrieval system without permission in writing from the author.

Although the author has researched all sources to ensure the accuracy and completeness of the information contained within this book, no responsibility is assumed for errors, inaccuracies, omissions, or inconsistency herein. Any slights of people, places or organizations are completely and totally unintentional.

ISBN # 978-0-9758649-2-0

Library of Congress Control Number: TXu 2-092-278

First Edition

Printed in the United States of America

Cover image:
Zapata Footprint
Dr. Don R. Patton
dpatton693@aol.com

Mom, this one is for you...

It was not often, back in the 60's and 70's, to have a parent who was passionately interested in science fiction, fantasy, and horror. I remember growing up watching television shows like Star Trek, One Step Beyond, Outer Limits, Twilight Zone, The Prisoner, The Amazing Kreskin, and The Sixth Sense and movies including 2001: A Space Odyssey, Planet of the Apes, Jason and the Argonauts, Chariots of the Gods, Godzilla, and the Thief of Bagdad. These shows fascinated me. They made me think deep, ponder alternative realities and consider possibilities that are many times regarded as being *outside of the box*.

Mom, thanks sharing your world with me and for opening me up to looking at life from a different point of view. I especially want to thank you for teaching me to boldly go where no one had ever gone before!

EVOL

Table of Contents

Foreword 1
Introduction 3
Chapter 1: The Ongoing Debate 9
Chapter 2: The Authors Of Myth................................ 20
Chapter 3: Who Are The Gods? 26
Chapter 4: The Birth Of Humanity 35
    Adam: The First Man 42
Chapter 5: From Ape To Man 48
    The Formation Of Behavior 57
Chapter 6: A Cognitive Shift 60
    Language.. 60
    Art 65
Chapter 7: The Fabric Of Society 70
    Love And Marriage 78
Chapter 8: All Things Sacred 84
    The God-King 84
    Divine Fluid 87
    Contact With The Dead 91
    Ritual Purification & Rebirth 92
Chapter 9: The Invisible World 96
    Manes, Lemures, and Larvae 98
    Ancestor Worship...106
Chapter 10: The Communion 108
    Finding God Through Chemistry...................... 114
    Animal Sacrifice: The Blood Ritual.................... 119

The Human Canvas 124
The Face of God 127
The Sacred Caribberie 129
The Ecstatic Experience: A Modern View 134
Chapter 11: Man or Myth – The Gods Revisited 140
Chapter 12: Body Modification 145
    Tattooing 146
    Scarification 153
    Ear Piercing/Earlobe Stretching 155
    Septum & Nose Piercing 158
    Labret Piercing /Lip Stretching 160
    Dental Modifications 162
        Teeth Filing 163
        Dental Inlays 165
        Tooth Ablation 166
        Tooth Staining 167
    Circumcision 168
        Subincision 171
    Cranial Deformation 173
    Initiation Rites 178
Chapter 13: 183
And It Doesn't End There 183
    Medicinal Plants 188
    Trepanation 192
Chapter 14: More Questions Than Answers 196
    A Journey Through Time 200
    The Million-Dollar Question 208
    Who Are We? 213

Foreword

There are so many books coming out that focus on an amazing site, new discoveries in the paranormal fields, and further discussions of alternative forms of history acknowledging advanced civilizations. Many, but not all of our books, fall into the same insular category. Such is the abundance of alternative research available. There is great danger that the seeker will be overwhelmed and be unable 'to see the forest but just one tree.' Big picture thinking is becoming a lost art that sorely needs a champion, and undeniably, Dr. Rita Louise has taken on that role.

By combining the major players in 'science and myth,' a combination for those who are led by the five senses would find contradictory at first glance, Dr. Rita has done something we could never equal. Trying to put together a big picture that accommodates two strands many would assume to be in opposition is fraught with many pitfalls. It could become too verbose and complex or descend into something so simplistic it would become an insult to both fields of endeavor. Dr. Rita has managed to straddle the divide. This book is without equal, so much so that when trying to find a comparison all I could come up with was a book many regard as the shining star which discusses the birth of rock and roll, Lillian Roxon's classic tome, Rock Encyclopedia.

This book is long overdue. It blends both sides of human endeavor both with style, insight, and clarity. It is pieced together in a cohesive narrative that leads on to a final question "Who Are We," where the answer has already been given. In Dr. Rita's journey through time, space and into the stars, each step forward is often accompanied by the realization that many popular facts, often held sacred as scientific truths, are captives to our inability to factor in the spiritual or a history deliberately hidden. In Dr. Rita's historical investigation she acknowledges both the benefits of scientific methodology and its inherent weakness in denying magic and the power of the spirits and Earth.

What Rita is seeking and finds, is the middle path where science's strengths and limitations are exposed and placed on the second rung of the human ladder. It is the "Invisible World" that provides the substance and setting that science is eternally subservient.

Knowing, in general terms, the lofty aims and poor track record of others who have tried to be so expansive and inclusive, I did fear the worst when I began reading this book. But within half a chapter I realized this was not a task, but an absolute joy to read. I learned so much and certainly added more to our understanding of the past many times over. It is a book that has drawn from sources across the globe and over extended periods. It succeeds at every level.

My only concern about this magnificent book is of a personal nature, in that we are in the process of doing something similar, compiling our own overview of the evolution of this planet and rise of hominids, with a heavy Original influence. Dr. Rita has set the bar so high with this book there is no way we can reach this standard. Our goal is simple and realistic. We can aim for second best and accept that this book is just too good and stands alone.

— Steven Strong and Evan Strong
authors of *Out of Australia: Aborigines,
the Dreamtime*

Introduction

Contemporary scientific circles assume that our myths and legends are flights of fantasy, the creative inventions of fertile minds or the product of someone's fanciful imagination. Some suggest that these stories help us to understand ourselves by incorporating concepts such as material creation, consciousness, the ego, the intellect and our spiritual connection with the divine. Others assert that ancient myths, unlike the stories told in the *Bible*, describe universal archetypes or planes of spiritual existence. They point to the fact that the celestial beings spoken of in these stories are rationalizations to explain the forces of the natural world or are stories to help us better understand our place in it. Accounts provided by some of the most seemingly backward cultures around the world, make it clear that they could tell the difference between fact and fantasy, a living breathing person and a non-corporeal spirit, an abstract concept and something that was right in front of their eyes.

Could the stories that come from our myths, legends and folktales be true? Is it possible for a group's history to remain intact over the eons? A story that made headlines in January of 2015 may prove that it can!

Nicholas Reid, a linguist at Australia's University of New England specializing in Aboriginal Australian languages, studied 18 traditional Aboriginal stories that describe coastal flooding in Australia. They came from a variety of regionally separated groups. The narratives recorded by early ethnographers tell of a time when the local people were able to walk to places that are now islands off the coast of Australia. The stories describe an era when the land was dry. They hunted emu and kangaroos in these regions that is until one day when the water rose and never receded again (Fig. 1). Remarkably, each legend studied told in effect same thing.

Figure 1 - Australian First People warrior.

> *In the beginning, as far back as we remember, our home islands were not islands at all as they are today. They were part of a peninsula that jutted out from the mainland and we roamed freely throughout the land without having to get in a boat like we do today. Then Garnguur, the seagull woman, took her raft and dragged it back and forth across the neck of the peninsula letting the sea pour in and making our homes into islands.*
>
> – Ancient Aboriginal Stories Preserve History Of A Rise In Sea Level, Nick Reid and Patrick D. Nunn

Introduction

To many, the above legend may just sound like a silly story, but researchers have equated this and other indigenous narratives to real events. Reid, working with geography professor, Patrick Nunn, was able to match elements of their ancient tales with geological changes to the land. These changes paralleled the narratives provided by the local inhabitants.

The unique context of their stories and the corresponding geological data lead Reid to believe their stories were based on personal observations and not invented. He concluded that the accounts were about 10,000 years old. At that time, sea level was 200 feet lower than where it is today. Sea levels rose inundating these coastal locations with water by the end of the ice age. *"It's quite gobsmacking to think that a story could be told for 10,000 years,"* Reid admits. *"It's almost unimaginable that people would transmit stories about things like islands that are currently underwater accurately across 400 generations."* So, as the story describes, the sea did come rushing in.

In the 1908 book, *Folklore As An Historical Science* by George Laurence Gomme, we find another example of how we have retained ancient concepts and carried them into modern times.

> *Immediately contiguous to the north side of the Roman road at Litlington, near Royston, were some strips of unenclosed, but cultivated, land, which in ancient deeds from time immemorial had been called "Heaven's Walls." Traditional awe attached to this spot, and the village children were afraid to traverse it after dark, when it was said to be frequented by supernatural beings.*
>
> *Here is subject for inquiry. Both words in the name are significant. Why the allusion to Heaven; why is a field called walls? The problem was solved in 1821, for in that year some laborers were digging for gravel on this spot, and they struck upon an old wall composed of flint and Roman brick. This accidental discovery was*

followed up by Dr. Webb, and the wall was found to enclose a rectangular space measuring about thirty-eight yards by twenty-seven, and containing numerous deposits of sepulchral urns containing ashes of the dead.

It was clear from the results of the excavations that here was one of those large plots of ground environed by walls to which the name of ustrinum [the site of a historical funeral pyre] was given by the Romans, a fact which was preserved in the name long after the site had lost every trace of its origin.

– Folklore As An Historical Science,
George Laurence Gomme

In my book, *ET Chronicles: What Myth And Legends Has To Say About Human Origins*, I present evidence, which suggests that the myths that have survived into the present are based upon true stories and actual events. It delves into our most ancient legends, the stories of the gods. It offers an in-depth look at the history of the Earth, starting with *in the beginning* and continues through the formation of man and the rise of civilization. It brings together both the mythic narrative and scientific finds into a synergistic whole. It draws its material from cultures including the Sumerians, the Greeks, the Maya, Native Americans, the Chinese, the Inca and the Aborigines of Australia and shows the unbelievable similarities in their oral and written traditions. It endeavors to present empirical evidence that the stories found around the world represent one consistent and unwavering record of our past. Taken as a whole, what it reveals about our history is astonishing.

As we move forward, I will be covering a number of topics that were discussed in this earlier text but will be looking at it from a different perspective. I will provide a brief synopsis of materials explored in detail within those pages and then move onto the new information. For the reader who is interested in delving into these topics further, I will refer them to the associated chapter within the book.

Introduction

Stepping Out Of Eden takes the concept of human origin to a whole new level. It explores our foundational beliefs, thoughts, actions, and deeds. It asks the question: why do humans act human? If you think about it, we do not behave like any other life form on the planet. Scholars contend that humanity evolved in small independent societies across the globe. They suggest that the time-honored traditions held by our ancestors have no bearing on who we are today. They advocate that the beliefs and values held long ago were left behind as we advanced socially, culturally and technologically. They overlook the fact that it is from these roots that we have come into being.

There is another aspect of the human experience that *Stepping Out Of Eden* explores. It delves into the notion of why do all humans have the same foundations beliefs. If you content yourself with saying, *"well Americans are vastly different from the Australian First People,"* you are missing the point. If instead, you compare what is considered human nature (something that is often regarded as part of our genetic make-up) with the warrior Klingons, the intellectual but unemotional Vulcans or the money lusting Ferengi of Star Trek, you can see that humans act *human* - but why?

Where did our founding beliefs come from? How far back in time were they instilled in us? Are they associated with the rise of civilization or do they have a deeper, more remote past.

Stepping Out Of Eden combines information from theological sources, the mythic record, and archeological finds to explore the essence of humanity. Most importantly, it delves deeply into the customs, rituals, and beliefs held by both ancient and modern indigenous cultures. Why look at aboriginal cultures? Because many of the traditions found sacred in one group are also revered by cultures thousands of miles away. Additionally, if members of modern indigenous societies can recall details of an event that occurred 10,000 years ago, then it only makes sense that the longstanding sacred traditions they embrace today would be remembered and reenacted in a more pristine form.

After that, with a bit of speculation on our part, we will endeavor to fit together the pieces that have been lost over time. It is from this vast library of information, which includes the *Bible* that we will learn about the origin of humanity and the nature of what it is to be human.

Chapter 1:
The Ongoing Debate

Does our genetic make-up determine our humanity? Is it our biological differences, our lack of body hair, the size of our brains, opposable thumbs or our ability to walk upright? Scientists spend countless hours investigating our biology but little time trying to figure out why we do the things we do, think the way we think and experience the world in the way we have. Do our traditions and customs, play a role in the formation of who we are? If so, how does it influence us? Could this be the reason why no other animal on the planet wears clothes, builds cities or believes in God?

Early anthropologists

Figure 2 - Illustration of the Decent of Man.

conjectured, based upon Darwin's *Theory of Evolution* that all life descended from a common ancestor, from simple organisms into increasingly complex forms through a series of genetic mutations – the survival of the fittest (Fig. 2). Random beneficial mutations that appear within an organism's genetic code are preserved and are passed on from one generation to the next. Over time, the accumulated slow, but gradual shift, in an organism resulted in an entirely new species. This process, according to the accepted scientific model, took place over extended periods of time, billions of years, through a slow and gradual process.

When researchers examine the archeological record, they are unable to explain how many of the drastic changes they have found occurred. For example, a strange genetic event happened in the plant kingdom at about the same time we started baking flatbreads. Wild einkorn wheat (Triticum monococcum) crossbred with a species of goatgrass (Aegilops speltoides) to produced a grain that is commonly known as emmer wheat.

Traditionally, if two species are genetically similar, cross-breeding can occur. Breeding across different species, however, produces sterile offspring. Hybrids can be found in the animal kingdom. Mules, zonkeys, yattle, ligers, and yakalo are all examples of infertile hybrid animals. The same genetic rules apply to the plant kingdom. But that is not what happened 30,000 years ago.

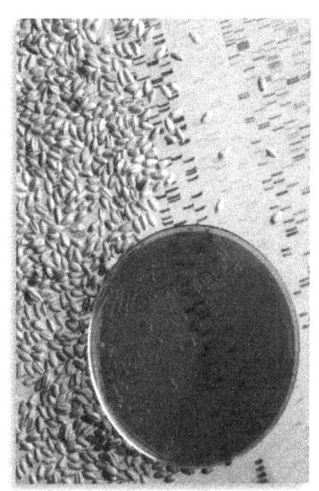

Figure 3 - Genetic engineering.

Genetically, einkorn wheat and goat grass each have 14 chromosomes (Fig. 3). If we call the 14 chromosomes structure of einkorn wheat AA and the 14-chromosome structure of goatgrass BB, when they combine, the genetic makeup of the

Chapter 1: The Ongoing Debate

resultant hybrid crop should have a mix of genes with a corresponding 14 chromosomes. This cross-bred hybrid plant, with half of its genetic material coming from each parent (AB), would be, like other hybrids, sterile.

Nevertheless, this is not what happened in the case of emmer wheat. Its genetic structure, instead of having the expected AB chromosomal mix, contains the full genetic structure from both parents (AABB). This combination of cellular materials, with its full complement of genes, restored fertility to the resultant plant. Surprisingly, only one twenty-eight-chromosome species of wheat can be found in nature: wild emmer. Grains of wild emmer, discovered at the ancient site of Ohalo II, date back to 17,000 BC.

The domestication of wheat, around 10,000 years ago, allowed our ancestors to move from a hunter/gatherer lifestyle to a more pastoral and agrarian one. It was during this time that a second miraculous genetic anomaly occurred. Modern bread wheat is a hexaploid organism, meaning it has six full sets of chromosomes. Sometime around 10,000 years ago, the newly develop emmer wheat (AABB) crossed with an unrelated form of wild goatgrass, (Aegilops tauschii (DD)) to produce a new grain whose genetic structure contained 42 chromosomes (AABBDD). This new species is commonly known as bread wheat today.

The mystery does not end there. Since the emergence of bread wheat about 10,000 years ago, the unlikely, yet successful, crossing of two distinct species of wheat has never happened again. Scientists continue to claim that nature was able to produce a series of fortunate genetic anomalies that ultimately transformed humanity, yet are still unable to explain how they occurred.

Scientists, at the labs of the International Maize and Wheat Improvement Center (CIMMYT), have been attempting to reproduce what is believed to have been a natural occurrence. *"We've been re-enacting in the lab what took place in nature nine-thousand years ago,"* stated researcher Richard Trethowan. Trethowan has been crossing wild goatgrass with a modern version of emmer wheat to produce a new form of bread wheat. At CIMMYT, however, chemicals are being used to induce hybridization and the chromosome doubling of these two distinct species. Interestingly, no wild forms of hexaploid (42 chromosomes) wheat exist on the earth.

It is not only in the development of modern wheat that we find unexplainable events occurring in the plant kingdom. The origin of maize (Indian corn) has intrigued historians and geneticists alike. The identity of maize's wild ancestor has long been a mystery. Scientists were at a loss to explain where it originated. Corn does not grow naturally on the planet. The appearance of a plant, with soft starchy kernels arraigned in long rows on a cob, appears abruptly in the archaeological record of the Americas. Evidence suggests that corn was part of their local diet about 9000 years ago. Milling tools, with maize residue on them, have been discovered in the *Xihuatoxtla* shelter of Balsas region of Southern Mexico that date back 8700 years.

Figure 4 - Teosinte plant in the wild. Image courtesy of Mbhufford.

Researchers, like Harvard professor Paul Magelsdorf, believe that early farmers domesticated a wild form of maize, which is now extinct. Evidence to support this theory has yet to be discovered. In the last few years, however, geneticists think they may have uncovered its source. Research indicates that the development of corn was a feat of genetic engineering.

Chapter 1: The Ongoing Debate

They believe that corn was intentionally developed from the wild grassy plant called *teosinte* (Fig. 4).

The confusion experienced in the past occurred because the seeds of teosinte do not resemble maize in its general appearance. Where one would expect to find an ear of corn, teosinte plants contain clusters of slender seedpods. Each seedpod contains 3 to 8 very tightly enclosed seeds. A hard, woody protective casing, called a *glume*, sheaths each of them. The glume allows the seeds to pass more easily through the digestive tract of animals, which aids in seed dispersal and helps to protect the seeds when they lay dormant during the winter.

Teosinte was initially classified as a different genus, but DNA analysis tells another story. It reveals a very close relationship to corn, one so close that the two plants can cross-pollinate and produce viable, not sterile, offspring. Because of a mutation to the *tga1* (Teosinte Glume Architecture1) gene, the glume of the teosinte seeds receded to form the now familiar cob and exposed the easier to eat kernels.

We see the same kind of unexplainable changes in our genetic heritage. For example, the *FOXP2* (Forkhead Box Protein 2) gene is not exclusive to human beings. Most multicellular organisms have it. It is associated with our ability to speak and use language. This gene has undergone three significant changes over the last 70 million years. Two of them are found exclusively in the human lineage. The mutation is also present in our *Neanderthal* cousins but is absent in Chimpanzees.

Another gene mutation associated with the rise of humanity is the *MCPH* (microcephaly primary hereditary) gene. The MCPH gene is responsible for the regulation of brain size. In early hominids, this gene did not vary for over 5 million years. Our brains were about the size of the great apes. It is believed, based upon the genetic diversity of this gene, that mutations to it originated around 2 million years ago. These genetic changes (so far six variations have been discovered) are believed to be responsible for the doubling of our brain size as is seen in the typical modern human brain.

We can only assume that *Neanderthals* possessed this same genetic structure as well.

Changes to our DNA did not end there. About 37,000 years ago, humanity began to express a version of the MCPH gene called *haplogroup D*. This version of the MCPH gene is the most common form found around the world except in Sub-Saharan Africa. The emergence of this gene, like earlier forms of the MCPH gene, parallel a significant change in humanity where its arrival correlates to the rise of behaviorally modern man and the *creative explosion*.

The most recent mutation associated with the human genome is the *ASPM* (Abnormal Spindle Microtubule Assembly) gene. The ASPM gene regulates the size of the cerebral cortex of the brain. This new version of the gene is estimated to have appeared somewhere between 5000 and 10,000 years ago. While scientists are still not sure how this gene affects us, its appearance during this time puts it at the advent of modern civilization.

The measured transition described in the Theory of Evolution begins to fall apart when you look closely at the timeline involved in the development of humanity. By 3.6 million years ago, a distant ancestor of modern man, *Australopithecus*, was already walking upright. This feature, according to researchers, took over 1 million years to surface in early hominids. *Australopithecines* had small brains, limited knowledge of tools and no vocal language.

In less than 2 million years, early man had obtained a group of traits that transformed him from being primate-like to looking and acting more like a contemporary man. *Homo erectus* had shed his body hair. Member of a group could speak to one another. They used complex tools, hunted animals and controlled fire. They show all of the signs of emerging modern culture. Scientists are still at a loss for how all of these dramatic changes could have occurred in such a short span of time. (ET Chronicles – The Age Of Man)

Darwin's observations set off a debate that has been going on for over 150 years. Called the creation-evolution controversy, the creation vs. evolution debate or the origins debate, a dispute between scientific and theological scholars about the origin of life quickly became heated. It only took a short time before a schism formed. The once widely held belief that God created us was replaced by a theory that was based on *empirical scientific fact*. The scientific community, in turn, viewed the traditional views held by Christians as pseudoscience.

Today, individuals who hold on to the belief that we were created by God and not via some natural mechanism are referred to as *Creationists*. Creationism teaches that the universe and all the life in it originated *from specific acts of divine creation*. Creationists do not attempt to explain God, his motives nor his processes, but put their faith in the words found in the *Bible*. Advancements in science, since Darwin proposed his theory, has caused competing models to emerge within the Creationist movement. Their views range from a literal interpretation of the *Bible* to the incorporation of particular scientific facts.

Young Earth creationists accept the biblical narratives as the true word of God and take what it says literally. They believe that God created the Earth within the last ten thousand years in a process that lasted six days. The date identified for creation is based upon Ussher's Chronology, which was established by the Archbishop of Armagh, James Ussher in the 17th-century.

Ussher derived his timeline by adding up the lifespan of early biblical characters and the later biblical kings. He deduced that the first day of creation began at 6 pm on Saturday, October 22, 4004 BC (Fig. 5).

The age of science was fast exploding after the release of Ussher's chronology. Ongoing finds in the archaeological and geological record suggested that that the Earth was tens, perhaps even hundreds of millions of years old. These discoveries brought Ussher's Young Earth theory under scrutiny and caused some to adopt a new form of creationism, *Old Earth creationism.*

Old Earth creationists believe that the Earth IS as old as scientists estimate. They think God played an active role in the

Figure 5 - 18th century illustration representing Ussher's timeline.

creation of the universe, the Earth and all life within it. They go on to explain how God performed countless acts of creation throughout history where he acted directly or as a guiding force behind his creations.

Progressive creationists, like Old Earth creationists, accept the scientific timetable for the age of the world. They also give credence to the role evolution plays in the development of life on the Earth. They believe that God created each kind of organism, not as the result of evolution, but as a series of separate acts of creation. They also think that *micro-evolution* took place. Micro-evolution involves the gradual accumulation of mutations leading to adaptations **within** a species. Progressive creationists contend that evolution counts for variations within a species but not for the creation and formation of a new species itself.

Archeologists began to unearth and catalog the bones of early man around the time Darwin proposed his theory of natural selection. The fossils discovered showed evidence of advancement from simpler to more complex hominid forms. The exemplars revealed a series of distinct beneficial changes that precipitated the advent of modern man. These changes, based upon their relative dating, occurred over extended periods. These finds supported the precepts associated with the Theory of Evolution.

Researchers, however, were unable to (and are still unable to) explain how these drastic changes occurred. They have scrambled for years hoping to discover the *missing link*, a set of archaic human bones that would provide conclusive evidence of our transition from ape to man. Despite their best efforts, this smoking gun has yet to be found. They assume that in time they will unearth it and prove to humanity once and for all that we did indeed evolve from a lower life form.

Their inability to produce the missing link has fueled the Creationist argument that the universe and all life in it originated from specific acts of creation and not from a slow and gradual process. They argue that the variation observed in our genetic makeup only goes to prove the hand of God at work.

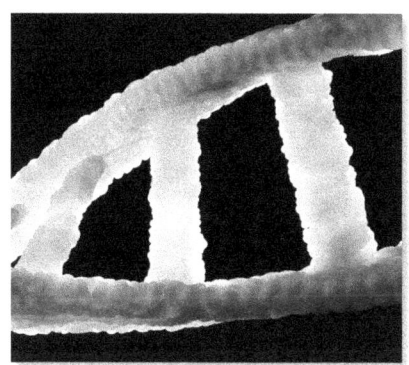

Figure 6 - DNA chromosome.

Recent studies into the human genome add to their argument. Geneticists suggest that the actual difference between our nearest living relative in the animal kingdom, chimpanzees and us, is a mere 5% of our total genetic makeup. Of our 23 chromosomal pairs, 18 pairs are virtually identical (Fig. 6). The most marked differences turn up on chromosomes 4, 9 and 12. Researchers into the human genome concede that the DNA of these genes does not appear in the same order as chimpanzees. In their own words, they state that *"these chromosomes display evidence of being 'remodeled."*

Think of it as you may, the creation story as portrayed in the *Bible* does offer something that should not be ignored. No matter where you look, regardless of which culture you come across, all of the stories of how we came into being are virtually the same. They state that **God** created all life on Earth, including humanity - period. While creationists do not look outside the *Bible* to support their claims, cultures from around the world support the fundamental beliefs held by creationists.

We find the familiar story of the creation of man in the *Bible* (Fig. 7). Genesis 1:27 states: *"So God created mankind in his own image, in the image of God he created them; male and female he created them."* The Bible, however, is not the only place that one can find this story. Countless ancient narratives detail the creation of man. The most common variations include making him out of clay or forming him out of the blood, bones or other genetic materials of a god. (ET Chronicles – The Age Of Man)

In the Aztec creation myth, Mictlantecutli, the God of the

Figure 7 - Detail of Michelangelo's Creation of Man.

Underworld, gave Xolotl instructions on how to create a man from the bone of one of the giants who had dwelt upon the Earth. The creation of man according to Chinese legend is associated with the goddess Nu Kua. The beautiful Chinese half woman, half dragon goddess Nu Kua emerged from the heavens to the Earth, and while sitting by a pool of water, she grabbed a handful of earth and created a creature in her image.

Several cultures also share stories of making more than one attempt to fashion humanity. These stories tell of the god's less than triumphant iterations until a final version is created. We find out in Sumerian mythology that numerous endeavors were made to shape the perfect man. The goddess Ninmah made six attempts each with poor results. The fertility god Ea worked on the seventh. The Mayan text, the *Popul Vul*, informs us that the gods tried three times to form humankind. They were finally successful when they made people out of colored corn, red, white, yellow, and black. (ET Chronicles – The Age Of Man)

World myth, upon examination, does not recount stories of a slow and gradual process. What we find are multiple accounts of the gods *creating* humanity. These stories also reflect the concept that several different methodologies were used until the perfect man was formed. Is it possible that what we have uncovered in the archeological record, the earlier forms of man, *Australopithecus*, *Homo habilis*, *Homo erectus* and *Homo neanderthalensis* are a record of the prototype versions of man as portrayed in myth?

Chapter 2:
The Authors Of Myth

Before we get into the meat of this topic, one thing to consider when evaluating our oral and written traditions is to identify who wrote the account. One way to help determine who penned these narratives is to look at the perspective through which the myth is told. Geraldine Woods, in her book *AP Literature & Composition for Dummies,* states: "*Literature provides a lens through which readers look at the world. Point of view is the way the author allows you to "see" and "hear" what's going on.*" An author's point of view can provide insights into his psyche which is the lens through which he views the world. Every author's voice is unique. It sets the tone of the work. Each author uses a different vocabulary, a different set of values and a different set of priorities as they relay their thoughts and ideas.

A soldier who survives a fierce battle in a war-torn country would describe his experiences differently than someone at home who sees the carnage on television. The soldier might see his participation as part of a day's work, as obtaining an objective or accomplishing a goal. An observer watching the late night news of these same events might feel horrified,

Chapter 2: The Authors of Myth

appalled or grief-stricken. Their thoughts, feelings, and perspective of what took place would be vastly different. We find a similar point of view in myths.

Myths can be broken down into two groups - early and late myths. Early legends tell of the origin of the world, the exploits of the gods and the creation of man. It details the god's elaborate and intricate plots, their ongoing violence as well as the scandals and conspiracies that took place in our prehistory. Their stories, instead of being ones of a loving kind creator, as portrayed in the *Bible*, is one filled with tales of their savage wars, their cruelty towards each other and their ongoing rivalries.

Figure 8 - The giant Titan Cyclops.

Greek legend, for example, informs us that Uranus ruled the heavens during the earliest period in mythological history. Together with his wife Gaia they had many children, the giant Titans (Fig. 8). Uranus both hated and feared his offspring, so he locked them up in the depths of Tartarus, the underworld. Gaia became incensed at the ill-treatment of her children and instigated a conspiracy to dethrone Uranus. Cronos, the youngest son of Uranus, lead the rebellion. Gaia supplied him with an adamantine sickle to use against his father. Cronos, together with his Titan brothers, overthrew Uranus and in a final act, Cronos castrated his father.

The Norse *Prose Eddas* also contain wild and somewhat gruesome stories of the early exploits of the gods. We learn, based on the narrative that the Aesir (the Gods of War) and the

Vanir (the Gods of Fertility) established a truce after a great war that raged between them. Both groups, to seal their peace, spat into a vat and from their saliva, Kvasir was born. Kvasir was a wise man who traveled the world giving knowledge to humankind. One day he paid a visit to the dwarves Fjalar and his brother Galar. The dwarves killed Kvasir and poured his blood into two vats, mixed the blood with honey and created *mead*. Anyone who drank the mead was endowed with wisdom and the power of poetry. The story goes on, and we find out that the giants, after a series of unfortunate and ill-intended events, end up getting the mead as reparation from the dwarfs. Odin, the head of the Aesir pantheon, through an act of trickery, steals the mead from the giants and takes it to share with the other Aesir gods.

When read, the narrator of these epic tales does not interact with the gods. He is right there, part of the action. His point of view is not one of awe and wonder or even shock, terror or fear. It reflects an attitude of familiarity with their ongoing bad behaviors. His viewpoint is not submissive or reverent, but more like he is part of the gang. There is a level of acceptance to the god's brutality. One we would expect to find a similar style of narration if a criminal gang member were to write about the exploits of his crew (Fig. 9). There is an inherent level of intimacy between the writer and the gods in early creation myths.

Figure 9 - Modern day street gang.

The gods bask in the limelight in our early narratives. Mankind, on the other hand, is but a footnote in the story and comes into our mythic history at the end of the book so to speak. They are rarely mentioned, and if they are, only the names of a few specific individuals are divulged.

A dramatic change is seen in an author's view, position, and interaction as we move into later myths. These narratives begin to emerge after the flood that devastated humanity. Later myths focus on the exploits of man. He occupies the primary position in these accounts. It seems clear that the stories of later myth were written and conceived by humanity. The commonalities found worldwide in creations myths disappear in later myths, which focus more on local beliefs and traditions.

Later myths contain several noteworthy characteristics, making them readily discernible from earlier ones. It is not uncommon to see a physical and emotional separation between the gods and man. The gods live in the heavens, the underworld or beneath the seas and man on the earth (Fig. 10). Many times they were described as being invisibly present in the world of man.

Figure 10 - God ruling from the heavens.

The gods were put on a pedestal, looked up to, prayed to and worshiped. In their time of need, our forefathers would call upon the gods for help. They prayed for the god's intervention and requested their assistance in their daily lives. We find this change of viewpoint, from being part of the story to adopting an attitude of reverence, in cultures around the world. An example can be seen in the Sumerian text *A tigi of Enki for Ur-Ninurta*.

Lord of complex divine powers,
Who establishes understanding,
Whose intentions are unfathomable,
Who knows everything! Enki,
Of broad wisdom,
August ruler of the Anuna,
Wise one who casts spells,
Who provides words,
Who attends to decisions,
Who clarifies verdicts,
Who dispenses advice from dawn to dusk!
Enki, lord of all true words,
I will praise you.

– A tigi of Enki for Ur-Ninurta

In the Native American *Prayer to Pachacmac*, we find a similar glorification and reverence to the gods.

O Pachacamac!
Thou who has existed from the beginning,
Thou who shall exist until the end,
powerful but merciful,
Who dist create man by saying,
"Let man be,"
Who defends us from evil,
and preserves our life and our health,
art Thou in the sky or upon the earth?
In the clouds or in the deeps?
Hear the voice of him who implores Thee,
and grant him his petitions.
Give us life everlasting,
preserve us, and accept this our sacrifice.

– Prayer to Pachacamac

Man, in these examples, looks up to the gods in prayer and admiration. The author's viewpoints toward the gods, even though the prayers were spoken worlds apart, are remarkably

Chapter 2: The Authors of Myth

similar. They are also reminiscent of prayers we might use today to commune with God especially in our time of need.

In these later accounts, the gods are portrayed as having a direct hand in human affairs. They would pick specific individuals upon whom they would imbue *favors*. The nature of these interactions, both good and bad, would determine whether a character's life was blessed or cursed. We consistently find the intervention of the gods into the lives of man in Greek mythology. Mankind seems more like pieces on a chess board. When humanity does interact with the gods, his attitude filled with awe and wonder.

In the Old Testament of the *Bible,* God also interacts with specific well-chosen individuals. Moses, in the book of Exodus, is one of these people. When God appears to him, his temperament is passive and obedient. His attitude throughout the passage is one of reverence and submission. The subservient posture, as displayed by Moses, is a widespread feature in all later myths.

If we, humankind, wrote these early tales, then what caused the change in our perspective? Why go from being part of the story to taking on an inferior, submissive position as later myths suggest? It also begs to broach the question, why does humanity feel a deep-seated reverence for an unseen god whom we still venerate today? What caused us to revere something which, as scholars suggest, is just a figment of our imagination? Could it be that there is more to god than meets the eyes?

Chapter 3:
Who Are The Gods?

We all share a collective belief in a creative force that is responsible for establishing all we see and experience. This presence, regardless of its form, is called *God* in the western world. God is viewed as the unknowable energy, force, being or consciousness that existed before our creation and caused our universe to come into existence. We often imagine God as a person. Many of us have given God a sex, making him easier to describe. Is he physical, vibrational, energetic, or pure consciousness? Ultimately, we are only able to grasp a small portion of who or what God is. From our limited vantage point, he is beyond our comprehension.

Many of us first learned of God from the *Bible*. We were taught that he underscores everything in our universe. The sun, moon, and stars. The mountains, rivers, trees, plants, animals even ourselves. He is beyond the reach of our senses, mind, and intellect. He is eternal, omnipotent and all-powerful. He is present everywhere. He is everything and nothing. God is the one who, through his unseen laws, supports, sustains, and governs all we encounter.

God, while perceived as a kind and loving spirit, is also portrayed as having a dark side. He, according to the *Bible*, is the one responsible for providing us with the laws we live by, establishing a covenant between himself and his people and

Chapter 3: Who Are the Gods?

freeing the Israelites from bondage. Texts also inform us that he is accountable for the destruction of Sodom and Gomorrah, the flood that wiped humanity off the face of the Earth and the plagues that brought a pestilence upon the land of Egypt.

Figure 11 - Michelangelo's Creation of Man.

God, as portrayed in the Judeo/Christian tradition, appears as an older Caucasian man sporting a white beard and wearing a white, flowing robe. How could we forget Michelangelo's captivating painting the *Creation of Adam*, where God's extended finger is touching the index finger of Adam, the first man (Fig. 11)? It is easy for those born into this tradition to see how we, according to Genesis 1:27, could look like God or he like us.

How did the writers of the *Bible* first learn of God? Where did they uncover tales of his works and deeds? What was their source of knowledge? Is the Biblical God the omnipotent creative force that underlies our existence as theologians claim, or is he something more?

Surprisingly, when surveyed, the limiting belief in a single all-encompassing God is only found in one spiritual tradition – in groups that claim a direct lineage to the biblical character

Abraham. The long-held conviction of a solitary benevolent creator does not pervade any other culture or religious tradition on Earth. Accordingly, the world, outside of Abramic traditions, was ruled by an assembly of gods with one god ruling supreme. The stories of their lives, times, triumphs and failures were commemorated in our written and oral traditions; the myths of a time gone by. Nevertheless, if our understanding of a supreme God is universal, what can we learn about him if we look at sources outside the *Bible*?

The underlying concept of god in indigenous traditions from around the world is the same regardless of the name associated with this presence. These traditions speak of an eternal and omnipotent creator. Even the most seemingly primitive cultures, irrespective of their local, have deep-set beliefs in an all-powerful deity. These groups keen understanding of god shocked early chronologists, historians, and missionaries who traveled to these newly discovered locations. They could not accept the local inhabitant's notion of a supreme being. *"How could the god of these savages be the same as the one and true God of Christianity?"*

Figure 12 - Cortés and La Malinche meet Moctezuma in Tenochtitlan November 8, 1519.

In the New World, when inhabitants from Mexico to Peru were asked to describe their creator god, they too describe him as being a bearded Caucasian man in flowing white robes. How could this be? From our history books, we know that the indigenous populations of the Americas never interacted with a white man until the arrival of the Spanish in the 1500s. What makes their claim even more amazing is that Native

Chapter 3: Who Are the Gods?

Americans do not grow excessive facial hair. A beard among their people is a rare occurrence.

On the day the Spaniards appeared off the shores of Mexico the Aztec believed them to be gods (Fig. 12). Their white-skinned, bearded leader, Cortés was wrongly identified as the Aztec supreme deity Quetzalcoatl. Cortés mistaken identity, as legend states, is the reason why the Aztec welcomed the Spanish conquistadors onto their lands with open arms.

Myth portrays the gods as having a physical form. Accounts suggest that the gods did not exist in the etheric realm but spent time on Earth where they actively participated in its formation and the development of life on it. Accounts suggest that they were seen, heard, felt, and touched. The gods, excluding the omnipotent Creator God, were perceived to be immortal beings, with lifetimes that extended far longer than our own. They, unlike the God of the *Bible*, could die or be killed and in many cases be brought back to life.

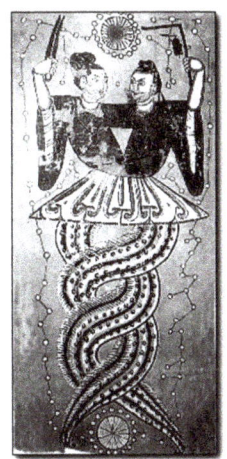

Figure 13 - Illustration of the Chinese gods Fuxi and Mawa.

The gods, however, are not always described as having human, much less Caucasoid, form. We only have to look at the original Greek pantheon to find gods depicted in strange ways. The progenitor gods Uranus and Gaia had many children, which included the giant Titans, the Hekatonkheires, a group of gods who had 100 arms and 50 heads, and the one-eyed Cyclope. Hindu and Buddhist traditions depict an array of gods with humanoid or partially humanoid form. For example, images of the sky god Indra illustrate him with four arms. Brahma, their chief celestial god, is shown with four heads. There are also descriptions of gods who take the form of snakes. Many are described as having the upper body of a man and the lower part of the body resembling a serpent (Fig. 13). Giants, dwarfs, and other monstrous creatures round out the pantheon of gods. (ET Chronicles – A God By Any Other Name)

Could these bizarre descriptions of the gods be true? Is our current perception of God a flight of fantasy? Could we have been deceived and our notion of a kind and benevolent, omnipotent creator god be fallacious? This just may be the case.

Let us take our notion of God one-step further. Many of us envision God as a being who can manifest whatever he desires at will. Like a magician, with one wave of his hand, it inexplicably comes into existence. As we delve deeper into the mythological record, we discover that the gods were able to do amazing things. One of their skills was shape-shifting, meaning they could change their outward appearance at will. This ability made it challenging for our ancestors to know what the gods actually looked like.

Stories are often told of the gods changing their form. In Greek mythology, Zeus is famous for this shape-shifting skill. He used it to seduce women. Forms he took included a white cow, a white bull, a swan, and a satyr. The ancient Greeks thought that seeing Zeus in his correct, unaltered form would cause instant destruction to mortals.

The Mayan god Quetzalcoatl is described as appearing both human and in the form of the feathered serpent. In Norse cosmology, both Odin and Loki are said to have changed their appearance, where they took female forms to tempt or spy on one another. Some First Nation legends speak of *skin-walkers*. These supernatural individuals could turn themselves into any animal they desire and then utilize the animal's abilities to enhance their own.

Instead of being able to magically transform themselves from one shape to another, as one would expect an omnipotent god to be able to do, the use of an object such as a ring, belt or feather was required to support their physical transformation. The creator god did not manifest these fantastic devices, the master builders, the giants, dwarfs and other creatures that lived in the earth's mountains, built them.

Chapter 3: Who Are the Gods?

Native American traditions suggest that a god must wear the pelt of a specific animal if they want to transform themselves into that creature. The Norse goddess Freya possessed a cloak of falcon feathers that allowed her to change into a falcon and soar through the skies. The Japanese spiritual beings, the Tennins, were able to descend to the Earth from the heavens. They appear in art wearing a colored or feathered kimono. Without their kimonos, they were unable to return to the land of the gods above. We find a similar story in the western Swan Maiden legends (Fig. 14). In Africa, tales recount rings or feathers being used by the gods to transform themselves. In these stories, magical words are often spoken preceding their transfiguration.

Figure 14 - Walter Crane's - The Swan Maidens.

Physical transformation was not the only wonder these magical objects bestowed upon the wearer. Plato, in his book *The Republic*, describes the mysterious *Ring of Gyges* that granted its owner the power to become invisible at will. Greek mythology also tells of a cap worn by Perseus, the *Helm of Darkness*, which made him invisible to the gods, heroes, monsters, and men.

These incredible stories of physical change can be found on every continent. If the gods, as we have been lead to believe, are omnipotent, then why would they need devices to change their shape or provide them with enhanced abilities?

The apparatus the gods used to alter their appearance are not the only pieces of unusual paraphernalia found in myth. Travel was not based upon the divine will of the gods, but instead via a flying carriage. Stories of golden, shining or magical celestial chariots pervade mythology. The gods, using one of these devices, are described as having the ability to transport themselves over incredible distances. These crafts flew through the air and sky. They were able to travel over land or sea and appeared to have no limitation in time or space. Drawn by celestial beasts, the gods used these vehicles to navigate the Earth and travel back and forth to the heavens.

Immortal horses, who were the offspring of the god of the wind, drew Zeus's chariot. Cronus' chariot was moved by two winged serpents while hippocampi pulled the chariot of the sea god Poseidon. The Norse *Prose Edda* informs us that two goats helped the mighty god Thor as he transited the skies. Freyr, another Norse god, travels in a chariot drawn by cats (Fig. 15). The Egyptian sun god Ra is often depicted riding in a solar barge across the sky.

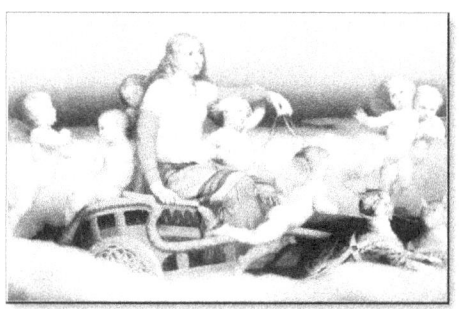

Figure 15 - Freyr on her cat drawn chariot.

The Native American tribe, the Hopi, talk about magical flying shields used by the gods to transverse the heavens. The gods, in India, travel in aerial chariots called vimana. We even encounter one of these awe-inspiring carriages in the biblical story of Elijah where Elijah ascends into the heavens on a fiery war chariot drawn by spirited horses.

Shapeshifting technology and flying chariots were not the only magical devices the gods had at their disposal. They also had magnificent but lethal weapons. The Archangel Michael is associated with his sword of truth. The trident, a three-pronged spear wielded by Poseidon, Neptune, Enki, and Shiva is celebrated for its ability to shake the Earth, where it causes earthquakes, tidal waves, and tsunamis (Fig. 16). The vajra, the deadly three-pronged weapon of the Sky God Indra, is said to emit thunderbolts. Other mythical armaments include Chun

Chapter 3: Who Are the Gods?

T'i's luminous bow, No-cha's Heaven-and-Earth bracelet, Innana's ankar weapon, Manco Capac's golden wand and the magical spike carried by Huang T'ien Hua. (ET Chronicles – The Gods And Their Toys)

Figure 16 - Poseidon wielding his three-pronged trident.

The stories of the gods and their miraculous toys at first glance seem colorful and far-reaching, yet it is evident these chronicles were essential to our ancestors. They were not some futuristic fictional narrative. They were central to their lives, their culture, and their traditions. They painstakingly memorized ancient accounts word for word and passed them down from generation to generation until they were finally immortalized in stone.

How did our ancestors come up with such intriguing chronicles in the first place? It is hard to believe that our forefathers could fabricate stories of celestial chariots, dangerous earth-shattering weapons, and magical transformational devices. Today when we hear thunder booming and see lightning transversing the night sky we can readily imagine a cosmic battle raging in the heavens. We have been exposed to, even if only on television or in the movies, the sound of gunfire, cannons, and bombs. We have also witnessed the devastating effect of a nuclear explosion. The information contained in these narratives benefits from a deep understanding of advanced technologies that are far beyond our predecessor's worldview.

It is human nature to take something that is known and transform it into something else. It is easy for us in this modern age to envision this possibility. We have been provided with images of extraterrestrial beings such as Vulcans, Romulans, Klingons, and Andorians (Fig. 17). We have, in the world of science fiction, traveled to galaxies far, far away on starships and battlecruisers. The measure of the technology we currently possess support these visions, making them seem plausible, if not now, but at some time in our future. Our ancestors did not have this luxury. Their stories come from a time when sticks and stones and bows and arrows were the most advanced technology they possessed. It seems inconceivable that they would be able to invent these narratives without a technological foundation to base it upon.

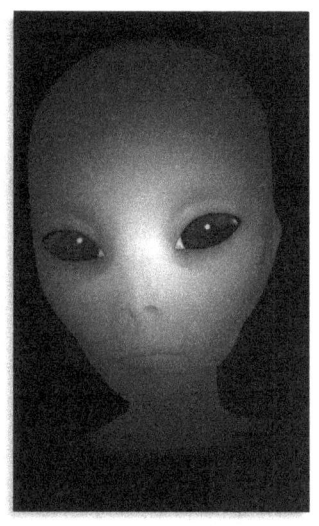

Figure 17 - Grey alien.

Taken from a different perspective, the universality of symbolism found around the world implies that the stories found in the mythic record were not born from the imagination of man. Could they instead be a memory of individuals our ancestors encountered? Was their interaction with the gods and their amazing technological feats so profound that their experience lived on in the psyche of humanity into the present? It is only through an actual encounter that a clear and specific portrayal of the gods, as we see in myth, could be made.

Chapter 4:
The Birth Of Humanity

It was once thought that the defining feature that separated us from apes was our enlarged cranial size. It was believed that with larger brains we were able to think, rationalize, have a sense of self and produce artwork – all the things associated with the development of society. As the field of archeology progressed, and more early human bones were resurrected from their ancient tombs, this notion was abandoned. Replacing it, as the first characteristic that defines the human (hominid) lineage is bipedalism, our ability to walk upright.

The facility of bipedal movement has a murky origin. In 2001, a group of French paleoanthropologists unearthed the skull of a 7 million-year-old early hominid called *Sahelanthropus tchadensis* in the west-central African country of Chad. Some researchers claim that *Sahelanthropus tchadensis* walked upright based on an anteriorly placed foramen magnum. The foramen magnum is the hole through which the spinal cord leaves the head. It is situated further forward in hominid skull than in an ape's. This positioning suggests that *Sahelanthropus tchadensis* held its head erect and could, therefore, walk upright. Many anthropologists remain skeptical about this species method of locomotion.

The 6 million-year-old *Orrorin tugenensis* also showed signs of adaptations to bipedalism. Archeologists based this conclusion on two bones, a femur and tibia, which were recovered from a site in Kenya. These bones exhibit features more closely associated with bipeds.

Figure 18 - Laetoli footprints. Image courtesy of Momotarou2012.

Clear signs of bipedalism first appear in the archaeological record with the discovery of the skeletal remains of *Australopithecus afarensis* who lived about 4 million years ago. In addition to physical changes that suggest upright locomotion, *Australopithecus afarensis* is attributed as the creator of a 27-meter long set of footprints discovered by Mary Leakey in 1976 in Tanzania, Africa. Called the *Laetoli Footprints* (Fig. 18), they provide convincing evidence for locomotion by a hominid in an upright posture. Researchers have concluded that the footprints were made by *Australopithecus* because it was the only hominid known to have existed in the region at the time.

Indications also suggest that with the advent of *Australopithecus* the manufacture and use of stone tools commenced. Two - 3.4 million-year-old animal bones with cut marks on them discovered in Ethiopia are believed to signify early stone tool use. This location has yet to yield the stone tools that may have been used to perform this function.

Chapter 4: The Birth of Humanity

Finds in Kenya, which dates to about 3.3 million years ago, conclusively show that early hominids began fabricating tools out of stones, which archeologists commonly refer to as *Lomekwian Tools*. One hundred and fifty artifacts have been unearthed that include, stone flakes, cores, hammers, and anvils and are the earliest example of devices made through the flaking process. Researchers have concluded that a sophisticated understanding of how rocks break along with fine motor skills was required to fabricate them efficiently.

The production of these early tools are typically allied with *Australopithecus afarensis;* however, the bones of another hominid species, *Kenyntropus Platyops* (the *flat-faced human from Kenya*), were found close to the find in Kenya and date to the same period. This discovery hints at the fact that *Kenyntropus Platyops* may have manufactured these early pieces of equipment. Whether *Kenyntropus Platyops* is a new hominin species or a separate species of *Australopithecus* is still under debate. What is exciting and cogent to our discussion are the newfound skills and abilities of these early ancestors.

Figure 19 - Oldowan style stone tool.

Australian anatomist and anthropologist, Raymond Dart, in the 1940's, suggested that *Australopithecines* might have employed an entire tool making tradition using the hard body parts of animals, their bones, teeth, and horns. His colleagues rejected his ideas sighting that there was a lack of evidence for the use of these materials as weapons or other types of tools. They determined that his theory was *"beyond the limits of scientific evidence."* In the same breath, they were able to conclude that we evolved from primates based upon a small scattering teeth and bones. How short-sighted his colleagues were, and in many cases, still are today.

Homo habilis, the *handyman*, our next stop in the development of modern man, lived 2.4 million to 1.4 million years ago. He was our first ancestor to show a significant increase in brain size and was the original hominid discovered who was undoubtedly associated with stone tools. *Homo habilis* fashioned the more advanced *Oldowan* style tool, a tradition they maintained for nearly a million years (Fig. 19). Erella Hovers, an archaeologist from the Hebrew University of Jerusalem, writing before the discovery of the Lomekwian Tools, concluded *"these tools appear to have been crafted by expert tool makers. By individuals who knew what they were doing."*

Some of these transitional humans evolved into a new, fully human species, commonly referred to as *Homo erectus* by 1.9 million years ago. *Homo erectus* was very successful in creating social technologies that allowed them to adapt to new environmental opportunities. We will be coming back to our discussion about the cultural advancements of *Homo erectus* in a moment.

Figure 20 – Acheulian style stone tool.

These early men started out using advanced or evolved Oldowan tool-making techniques, but by 1.5 million years ago, they began a new tool making tradition now referred to as *Acheulian* (Fig. 20). Several researchers split the *Homo erectus* lineage into two species, *Homo ergaster* (working human), and *Homo erectus* (upright human). The fossils of *Homo ergaster* are, according to *the authorities,* somewhat earlier than those of *Homo erectus* and have been found primarily in Africa, while the remains of *Homo erectus* are widespread in Africa, Asia, and Europe. (For simplicity sake,

Chapter 4: The Birth of Humanity

these two species will be referred to as *Homo erectus* unless otherwise specified.)

The exact descent of *Homo erectus* is convoluted at best and in recent days, ever-changing. History books tell us that the species *Homo habilis* was the direct predecessor to the later *Homo erectus*. Recent discoveries near Lake Ileret in Kenya are challenging this widely accepted belief. Ancient bones found in the region show the two species, *Homo habilis* and *Homo erectus* living for close to 500,000 years together in the same lake basin and may represent separate lineages from a common ancestor. An alternative explanation academics propose is that a subgroup population of *Homo habilis* became the ancestor of *Homo erectus*, with the balance of *Homo hablis* remaining unchanged.

The confusion does not end there. The surprising discovery in 1991 of a human jaw and teeth showing anatomical similarities to *Homo erectus* adds another twist to our ancestry. Before its discovery at Dmanisi, in the Republic of Georgia, everything seemed clear to anthropologists. The origin of humanity had taken place some 2.5 million years ago on the African continent. Then a migration of *Homo erectus* from Africa to Eurasia occurred sometime between 600,000 and one million years ago. Today, the discoveries in Dmanisi are challenging the fabric of our beliefs. It is also testing the accuracy of the much coveted *Out Of Africa Theory*.

Since its initial discovery, by archeologist David O. Lordkipanidze, five skulls, five mandibles, twelve isolated teeth and about fifty skeletal bones have been found. Also recovered from this location were a collection of Oldowan style stone tools. The bones display a species with primitive but distinct features often associated with the *Homo* lineage.

What makes the discovery at Dmanisi a potential game changer is that the bones and other artifact bearing deposits (stone tools, animal bones, etc.) were found directly over a layer of volcanic basalt, which conclusively dates these relics to about 1.8 million years ago. The secure age of the Dmanisi finds put a crimp into the Out of Africa Theory because these artifacts date to a time before *Homo erectus* appears in the

East African fossil record. It also brings into question the claim that the migration of the first *Homo* group outside of Africa could not have taken place earlier than 1 million years ago.

The discovery at Dmanisi has brought the supposition of Africa as the cradle of civilization under harsh scrutiny. Earlier finds, such as the ones discovered on the island of Java in 1891, *Java Man*, date to between 1.9-1.6 million years ago. The thought that *Homo erectus* could have lived in Java during such an early period was initially dismissed but is now being revisited in academic circles. The finds in the Republic of Georgia lend credence to the times associated with the Java Man remains and for the existence of *Homo erectus* in Asia at such an early date (Fig. 21).

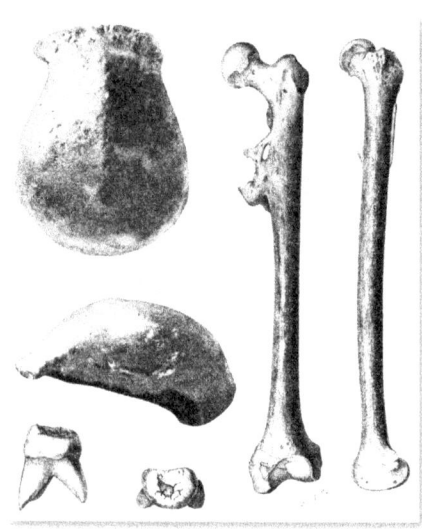

Figure 21 - Illustration of the three main fossils of Java Man found in 1891–92.

Some, based on this new evidence, suggest that *Homo erectus* evolved in Eurasia and then migrated to Africa. They occupied the Dmanisi site around 1.8 million years ago, which is about the same time or slightly earlier than earliest evidence recovered in Africa. Professor Lordkipanidze, the primary archeologist from the Dmanisi site, proposed that *Homo erectus* may have evolved in Eurasia from the more primitive Dmanisi population and then migrated back to Africa where they eventually gave rise to *Homo sapiens* – modern man.

An alternate theory tied to the new finds at Dmanisi proposes that either *Australopithecines* or an unknown species of *Homo* migrated out of Africa before *Homo ergaster* evolved.

Chapter 4: The Birth of Humanity

They suggest that the populations found at Dmanisi represent a missing link in the evolution of *Homo erectus and Homo ergaster*.

Amusingly, in the early part of the twentieth century, it was understood that humans evolved in Asia. This idea was conceived, based on the Theory of Evolution, that humans were more closely related to gibbons and orangutans. Early anthropologists suggested Southeast Asia as the cradle of civilization because this is where these apes live. In 1925, the discovery of a young hominid (*Australopithecus africanu*), the *Taung Child*, by quarrymen in Taung, South Africa provided the first evidence of an early fossil link between the apes and man. It was proposed, based on this find, that Africa was indeed the cradle of humanity. This bold assertion was dismissed at the time. Additional discoveries over the years, especially in the eastern part of Africa, cemented the concept that the African continent was the location of human origin.

There is yet another challenge facing proponents of human evolution as we move into modern times. There is little agreement about what name to give hominin remains after the age of *Homo erectus*. The evolutionary dividing line that separate modern humans from archaic humans and archaic humans from *Homo erectus* is unclear. As a result, they are all lumped together and given the label of *archaic Homo sapiens* or just *Homo sapiens*.

Some taxonomists consider archaic and modern humans separate distinct species and refer to them as *Homo Sapiens*, *Homo rhodesiensis*, *Homo neanderthalensis* and *Denisova hominin*. Recent DNA evidence has put a wrinkle into our understanding of early man. Genetic testing comparing the full genomes of *Neanderthals* and modern humans has determined that most Europeans and Asians have between 1 to 2 percent *Neanderthal* DNA in them. Indigenous sub-Saharan Africans, on the other hand, have very little or none. Modern populations from southeastern Asian islands share genes with *Denisovans*.

These finds indicate that interbreeding occurred between these diverse populations. It also provides compelling evidence that *Neanderthals* and *Denisovans* were not separate and distinct species but a subspecies of *Homo sapiens*. This newfound information has caused taxonomists to reclassify early modern humans as *Homo sapiens sapiens, Homo sapiens heidelbergensis, Homo sapiens neanderthalensis* and *Homo sapiens ssp. Denisova*, from which modern man emerged.

Adam: The First Man

Regardless of if you are a creationist or support the precepts associated with the Theory of Evolution, one matter we must address is when did we become human? When did we transition from ape to man? When was that magical moment in time? There are our physical characteristics as we have just explored, but when did we gain a sense of self and a level of consciousness? Do we point to the advent of *Homo sapiens sapiens* and the *Cultural Revolution* that occurred some 40,000 years ago as the line that separated us from the animal kingdom? Perhaps it was the advent of civilization and the formation of the city/state. We assume that Adam and Eve, once created held all of the hallmarks of society and culture, but what if that assumption is wrong?

Insights into this date, the date of the *first man*, may be garnered from the mythical record as well as archeological evidence. The first piece of subjective evidence comes from the *Bible* itself. Adam and Eve, after consuming fruit from the Tree of Knowledge, were expelled from the Garden of Eden. As they depart, we are informed: *"And Jehovah God proceeded to make long garments **of skin** for Adam and for his wife and to clothe them. Jehovah God then said: "Here the man has become like one of us in knowing good and bad."* - Genesis 3: 21-22.

Chapter 4: The Birth of Humanity

Did humanity gain a level of consciousness with the eating of the fruit of knowledge? Is this what set us apart from the rest of the animal kingdom our ability to differentiate between good and bad, right from wrong? One thing we do know is as early humans spread throughout Eurasia. The cold climate of their new environment suggests that they wore clothes made of animal skins to keep themselves warm.

Additional suggestive evidence comes from the myths and legends of India. In Hindu cosmology, religious texts inform us that their supreme god Vishnu incarnated on the Earth nine times in a variety of forms. Called avatars, his first three incarnations were of animals. There was Matsya the fish, Kurma the turtle and Varaha, the boar. His fourth embodiment was as Narshimha, the half man, half lion hybrid. His next five incarnations took on human form and were Vamana, Parashurama, Rama, Krishna, and Buddha. According to Hindu tradition, the avatars Vamana, Parashurama and Rama lived during the *Treta Yuga*, a period that began 2,165,000 years ago and extended until about 869,000 years ago. It is with Rama who lived near the end of the Treta Yuga that our story begins.

Rama, the seventh incarnation of Vishnu, is a popular figure in Hindu mythology. The book that chronicles his life, the *Ramayana*, is a time-honored classic. It tells of a time when the gods flew on ships through the air (vimana) and of giants who walked the Earth. Rama, according to the *Ramayana*, was sent into exile because of a promise his father made to his stepmother many years before his birth. His brother Lakshmana and his wife Sita joined him.

Through the course of a number of unfolding events, the 10-headed demon god of Lanka, Ravana, kidnaps Sita, Rama's wife. Rama discovers that Sita was being held captive on the island of Lanka. In an attempt to rescue her, he assembles an army of Vanara to help him battle the demon god. Rama, unable to move his massive forces across the open ocean to Ravana's island home, was advised by a sea god to build a bridge across the water. He enlisted the help of the Vanara for its construction.

The Vanara built a causeway between mainland India to the island of Lanka (Fig. 22). The bridge, constructed out of rocks and boulders, was 100 leagues in length. Once completed, it allowed Rama to transport his army across the ocean where they defeated Ravana and rescued Sita.

With the basis of the *Ramayana* revealed, we will turn our attention to the additional evidence that supports its connection to the creation of the first man during the Treta Yuga. The *Ramayana* tells us that before the birth of Rama, Vishnu sent the heavenly gods and goddesses down to the Earth to mate with the planet's apes and bears. (Some interpretations suggest that these animals were not monkeys in the literal sense but in the semblance of monkeys.) They were asked to have relations with these earthborn creatures to produce an army that would ultimately help Rama defeat Ravana. These *ape-men*, the *Vanara*, because of their semi-divine origin, possessed a portion of the skills and abilities of their godly shire, including increased strength, bravery, and intellect.

Figure 22 - Land bridge that connects mainland India to island of Sri Lanka. Image courtesy of NASA

Interestingly, we find a parallel, though less comprehensive myth written in the pages of the Old Testament of the *Bible*. In Genesis 6:4, not much after the creation of Adam in the Garden of Eden, we learn: *"There were giants in the earth in those days; and also after that, when the sons of God came in to the daughters of men, and they bore children to them, the same became mighty men which were of old, men of renown."*

Chapter 4: The Birth of Humanity

The narrative offered by this *Bible* verse does not provide any clues as to why the Sons of God came to the Earth; however, the apocryphal *Book Of Enoch* suggests that the sexual relations between the gods and man was a sinful act. *"And all the others together with them took unto themselves wives, and each chose for himself one, and they began to go in unto them and to defile themselves with them, and they taught them charms and enchantments, and the cutting of roots, and made them acquainted with plants."* - Book of Enoch 1:7. It is impossible to tell, based on so few surviving accounts, if this union was divinely inspired as suggested in the *Ramayana* or a torrid and sinful act as seen in this Judeo/Christian tale.

There is a funny thing, however, that happened during the Treta Yuga around 1.5 million years ago. It was the advent and rise of our progenitor *Homo erectus* (Fig. 23). Homo erectus displayed a series of genetic traits that were not present in earlier hominid groups. They

Figure 23 - Reconstruction *of Homo erectus*.

possessed modern human-like body proportions. Their brain size had increased. They lost their body hair. They could speak and use language. (ET Chronicles – The Age Of Man)

In addition to these physical changes, Homo erectus lived a multifaceted life. Their ability to use and manufacture complex stone tools had evolved. They were the first to display clear signs of a sophisticated social structure and the rudiments of culture as we know it. There is evidence suggesting they lived in small communities in a hunter/gatherer society, using oval-shaped huts as a temporary shelter. The formation of a cooperative society and its associated culture implies that a series of rules and regulations were required to help navigate the diverse population. We will be delving deeply into this concept as we move forward.

A substantiation of culture among *Homo erectus* populations comes from the toothless mandible of an old man. It is noteworthy because the old man lived for a relatively long time after wearing out and losing his teeth. Not only were all of his teeth missing, but nearly all of the tooth sockets were smooth and had filled in with boney tissue. Some believe that this indicates the man had lived for many years despite being wholly toothless and suggested to Professor David Lordkipanidze, a paleoanthropologist and the director of the museum in Tbilisi, that social organization based on mutual care existed.

In addition to the dramatic physical and cultural changes associated with *Homo erectus*, it was the first group to demonstrate an unmistakable ability to control fire. Trite as this skill may sound, it is critical to our ongoing dialogue and the dating of the first man.

The earliest suggestive evidence of fire being used by humans was found at two sites in Kenya and date back 1.5 million years. The first substantive verification that fire was used for cooking was uncovered at the *Wonderwerk Cave*, which is near the edge of the Kalahari Desert in South Africa. Found in the sediment was the ash of burnt grass, leaves, brush and bone fragments. Exhumed from the Chinese site of *Zhoukoudian* were charred bones and fire-altered stones, which provide further confirmation for the early use of fire. This site dates to around 780,000 years ago.

Where did we learn of fire? According to the mythological record, we got it from the gods! The gift of fire is one of the oldest and most consistent myths found around the world. In Greek mythology, the Titan god Prometheus stole fire from Mount Olympus and gave it to the human race. Prometheus, because he went against the will Zeus, was punished for his deceitful act. We find a similar story in Norse cosmology where the devious god Loki provided humanity with fire. Like

Chapter 4: The Birth of Humanity

Prometheus, he was also punished. In the Pacific Islands, Maui, a mischievous Polynesian god, stole it. In Japan, it was a tricky fox and in the Americas, a sly coyote.

Figure 24 - Early hunter/gatherers sitting by campfire.

If humanity came into existence 40,000 years ago or even 200,000 years ago, as some suggest, why create a myth of the gods giving humankind fire? People, by this point in our history, would have been using fire to cook their food and warm themselves on a cold winter's night for well over 1 million years (Fig. 24). It only makes sense if the advent of humanity was much further back in time.

Was Adam, the first man, a form of the early toolmakers represented by the hominid *Australopithecus* who lived about 4 million years ago? Is it possible that, as recorded in the biblical narrative as well as the Ramayana, that Eurasia was the location where the gods had relations with primitive humans? Are *Homo erectus'* advanced skills due to the union of gods and man? Did this union take place during the Treta Yuga as the Ramayana suggests?

Finally, was the merging of our DNA with the gods what spurred on the substantial advancements seen in this group, created our sense of self and encouraged the development of culture and society? Was this infusion of genetic materials enough to turn us around or was there an intervening event that changed us from being animal-like to becoming the people we are today? White, black, red or yellow, male, female, young or old, the difference between humans, *Homo sapiens sapiens*, and any other living creature on our planet are vast and distinct.

47

Chapter 5:
From Ape To Man

Researchers discovered, through the study of children who from a very young age have lived isolated from human contact (feral children), that social skills are not hardwired into our brains (See sidebar: *Victor: The Wild Boy Of Aveyron*). They determined that these attributes are a series of learned skills and behaviors and are not part of our genetic programming. If a puppy is taken away from its mother and fostered with human parents, it will still act like a dog, a cat a cat. This is not the case with humans. Human children, when cut off from society, do not automatically take on a more rudimentary form of humanity.

Daniel Griffin in his article Nature vs. Nurture, tells us that *"we pickup all of our skills and behaviors by watching, imitating and listening to others."* He goes on to state, *"People act as they do because they learned to be the people that they are."* These traits, like our DNA, get passed down, one generation to another, not as the result of biology, but as a result of conditioning. Katie Langloh Parker in her book The Euahlayi Tribe; A Study Of Aboriginal Life In Australia notes *"Even the smallest black child who can talk seems full of knowledge as to all his relations, animate and inanimate, the marriage taboos, and the rest of their complicated system."*

Victor: The Wild Boy Of Aveyron

The year was 1797 when hunters in Southern France found a naked, filthy boy living in the woods near Saint-Sernin-sur-Rance. He was observed walking on all fours, would pounce on small animals and then eat their raw flesh. The boy was a feral child.

A feral child is a young boy or girl who, beginning at an early age, lives for an extended period isolated from human contact. These hapless youths were lost, deserted or were kept isolated and away from other people. Their link to the civilized world of humanity, in each of the over 100 reported cased, was severed.

The boy emerged from the woods on January 8, 1800, of his own accord and was placed by local authorities into a hospital. The boy was thought to be 12 years old when he was discovered. He was eventually placed under the care of Dr. Jean Marc Gaspard Itard a young medical student. Itard began work to rehabilitate the youth. He believed that with the right care the boy, whom he named Victor, would become a normal member of society, regaining his humanity.

Victor had a keen sense of hearing and smell, like the animals who reared him, but what Itard came to realize was that Victor lacked a sense of self-awareness. If handed a mirror Victor was unable to recognize his reflection and would look for the child he saw in the mirror behind it. Using a form of sign language, Itard endeavored to teach the boy a means of communication. Victor showed real signs of progress in the beginning. He quickly learned some simple French words and was also able to order the letters of the alphabet.

Victor showed little signs of advancement after this initial development. Itard believed that he was able to imitate some of the words he heard but was never able to develop sentences or understand the rules and principles that govern sentence structure. Itard concluded there was little he could do to restore a sense of humanity to this young lad.

It was found, in the authenticated cases of feral children, that a child who had contact with adults until a later period in their lives had formed the basic building blocks of language. Their transition back into society, while not perfect, was vastly improved over Victor's recovery. Even with these children, their ability to fully conform to societal norms was always impaired.

A child, starting at birth (although there are those that contend that this conditioning begins in the womb) is continually being educated and guided by adults. If these early periods of learning are infringed upon, our ability to become indoctrinated into the status quo will be impaired. The developmental issues associated with Victor, and the other feral children, opens the door to the question, what makes us human?

Myth suggests there was a precipitating event that began us down the road to humanity. We can find some interesting insights in several ancient tales. These accounts indicate that we, or at least several specific individuals, were provided an education. One of the oldest written narratives that detail our early learning comes from the Sumerian *Epic of Gilgamesh*. In it, one of the leading characters, Enkidu, is described as such:

> *Aruru washed her hands, she pinched off some clay,*
> *and threw it into the wilderness [the wilderness = the edin:Sumerian].*
> *In the wildness(?) she created valiant Enkidu,*
> *born of Silence, endowed with strength by Ninurta.*
> *His whole body was shaggy with hair,*
> *he had a full head of hair like a woman,*
> *his locks billowed in profusion like Ashnan.*
> *He knew neither people nor settled living,*
> *but wore a garment like Sumukan.*
> *[Sumukan: the god of the wild animals, often assumed to indicate that Enkidu is wearing ragged animal-skins.]*
> *He ate grasses with the gazelles,*
> *and jostled at the watering hole with the animals;*
> *as with animals, his thirst was slaked with (mere) water.*
>
> –The Epic of Gilgamesh, Tablet I

The demigod, Enkidu (Fig. 25), formed of clay and from the loins of his godly shire Ninurta, the God of Thunder, Lightning and the South Wind, knows nothing of civilization

Chapter 5: From Ape to Man

and the workings of society. He lives with and acts like the animals of the field, wearing only animal skins. The local inhabitants, concerned by his excessive strength, a trait handed down to him from his father; call on the mighty Gilgamesh for help. Gilgamesh recruits the help of Shamhat, a priestess of Ishtar, to lure him in.

Figure 25 - Sumerian cylinder seal depicting Gilgamesh and Enkidu.

It was common during this era for a temple priestess to have relations with men. Shamhat using her beguiling skills entices Enkidu to come to her. After six days and seven nights with Shamhat, he is completely transformed. The animals that had been his friends in the past dart off and distance themselves from him. Shamhat tells Enkidu that he now has wisdom - that he is like a god. As the story continues, we soon find out that Shamhat gives Enkidu civilized clothing to wear and keeps teaching him the basics of societal life.

In India, one of the chief characters of the *Ramayana* is a Vanara called Hanuman (Fig. 26). He is the son of Vayu, God of the Wind and is named explicitly in this epic tale. Legend tells us that Hanuman was a wild child. He wanted to educate himself. He sought out the Sun God Surya to teach him the scriptures. Hanuman, under his tutelage, mastered the Vedas and was said to speak in the way of the Brahmin.

Figure 26 - Hanuman The Hero Vanara from the Ramayana.

We find a similar narrative in the tale of the beloved Chinese Sun Hou-Tzu. Created by the god Yu Huang to "*complete the wonderful diversity of beings engendered by Heaven and earth*" the monkey Sun Hou-Tzu set on the path of discovering the means to become immortal. He gradually took on human traits in his eighteen-years of searching. Legend tells us that he always looked like a monkey but had eventually become civilized.

Surprising as this may sound, myth indicates that our education and training was not a one-time thing but took place over the course of human history. Sumerian records inform us there was a time when the people of Sumer lived like beasts and wild animals in a lawless manner. Then from the Erythraean Sea, an animal endowed with reason appeared. Called *Oannes*, records described him as having the shape of a fish, but underneath the body of a man (Fig. 27). The Oannes interacted with humanity, according to the Babylonian priest Berossus, six times, three times before the deluge and three times after. He taught them, over the course of his visits, how to construct houses and build temples. He instructed them on seeds of the earth and helped establish their laws. The Oannes taught them in everything that *humanized* mankind.

In Greece, legend tells us that it was only after our interaction with gods such as Prometheus

Figure 27 - Ancient artistic representation of the Oannas.

Chapter 5: From Ape to Man

that humanity learned how to work with metal and grow crops. They believed that everything associated with the conveniences of *modern life* originated from the gods. In his book, *Myths and Legends of Ancient Greece and Rome* by E.M. Berens, we learn:

> *Like the wild plants and flowers, he was supposed to have had no cultivation, and resembled in his habits the untamed beasts of the field, having no habitation except that which nature had provided in the holes of the rocks, and in the dense forests whose overarching boughs protected him from the inclemency of the weather.*
>
> *In the course of time these primitive human beings became tamed and civilized by the gods and heroes, who taught them to work in metals, to build houses, and other useful arts of civilization.*
>
> – Myths and Legends of Ancient Greece and Rome, E.M. Berens

    The gods in Australia taught the local people how to gather edible roots using digging sticks. They taught the warriors how to use boomerangs to hunt. They even instructed the natives in the rites and ceremonies their communities were to follow. The task of civilizing humanity, in Egypt, is linked to the god Osiris. He transformed them from their former barbarous life and taught them to cultivate the fruits of the earth, provided them the laws to live by and instructed them in the rites, worship, and homage due to the gods. Egyptian historian Manetho, who lived during the 3rd century BC, identifies the *Egregori*, the Watchers for teaching the priests and pharaohs.

    The god Itzamna, according to the Maya, invented the character letters in which they wrote their books and used to carve on their monuments. He gives them the calendar in which to track time. He taught them the virtues of healing plants and the rites and rituals they could use to please the gods. The Algonquin attribute this to the god Michabo. He taught them how to perform the sacred ceremonies, how to hunt, fish and write. He instructed them about which roots and plants were good to eat and which could be used as medicine. In Peru, the god Viracocha taught people which plants were good for food, which for medicine and which were deadly. The Aztec identify the god Quetzalcoatl as the teacher of humanity while the Chinese point to Shen Nung.

Figure 28 - Manco Capac.

The Inca attribute their education to Manco Capac who instructed them in the art of civilization (Fig. 28). His wife Mama Ocllo taught woman domestic tasks such as the art of spinning and weaving. The Celts also held a similar belief regarding the role of the gods and the education of humanity. Like the Inca, they share a tale of how a goddess from the underworld gave flax seeds to a local cow herder. The cow herder planted the seeds in a nearby field. After the crops had withered and the seeds were ripe, the goddess reappeared and showed him how to prepare the flax. She then taught his wife how to spin and weave the fibers into cloth.

In the *Book Of Enoch*, it is *God* and his messengers the angels who teach Enoch, the great-grandfather of Noah the workings of the heavens and earth. In this text, we also discover one of the first acts of the Sons of God after their union with the Daughters of Man. These heavenly beings teach their offspring. *"and they taught them charms and enchantments, and the cutting of roots, and made them acquainted with plants."* - Book Of Enoch 1:7. Could this, like the devious exploits of Prometheus and Loki giving humanity fire, have been a sacrilegious act?

Chapter 5: From Ape to Man

It seems clear, from our ancient legends, that humanity was a pretty dumb lot. The gods, according to these narratives, gave us everything that underlies society. This education included information, which formed the very foundation of each and every civilization on Earth.

Could this have happened to us? Were we taught the rudimentary skills associated with civilization?

For over 40 years, experiments have been conducted whose goal is to teach chimpanzees and apes how to communicate with us. These apes were trained to use sign language, visual symbols or work with a computer program that converts visual symbols into a synthetic voice (Fig. 29). One chimp named Washoe understood how to utilize hundreds of sign letter words. When a 10-month-old chimp named Loulis was placed in her care, to the astonishment of her handlers, she quickly and automatically began teaching him some simple signs.

Figure 29 - Kanzi talking to researcher.
Image courtesy of William H. Calvin, PhD.

In another experiment, a bonobos chimp named Pan-Banisha had developed a vocabulary of over 3000 words. She was able to construct complete sentences in her conversations. She was even able to let her handlers know when she wanted a Starbuck ice coffee – *"Please can I have an iced coffee."* Researchers noticed that her son, Nyuota, was even more integrated into human society. Nyota, as a second-generation bonobo, lived alongside humans his whole life. They believe that his grasp of the human language is even more sophisticated than his mother's.

What is even more astounding is that at the Stone Age Institute researchers Nicholas Toth and Kathy Schick began teaching Pan-banisha and her half-brother Kanzi how to use and make stone tools. They learned how to produce sharp-edged flaked stone tools that they used for cutting activities. Charles Choi, a writer for *Inside Science,* informs us:

> *The researchers challenged Kanzi and Pan-Banisha to break wooden logs and to dig underground, tests similar to tasks the apes might have to carry out to get food in the wild. To break the logs – an act similar at cracking open bones to get at marrow – the scientists not only saw these apes use rocks as hammers or projectiles to smash their targets, but also observed them either rotating stone flakes to serve as drills or use the flakes as scrapers, axes or wedges to attack slits, the weakest areas of the log. To root into hard soil, these bonobos used both unmodified rocks and a variety of handmade stone tools as shovels.*
>
> – *Inside Science*, Charles Choi

The simple stone tools they created are comparable to Oldowan stone flakes tools that were manufactured by *Homo habilis*. Conventional science postulates that it took early man millions of years to be able to accomplish this feat. In the work done by the Stone Age Institute, it only took ten years for Kanzi and Pan-Banisha to master the task of creating and using stone tools.

Recent reports indicate that Loulis has learned how to construct and start fires to cook his own food. Now granted he was provided with a box of matches to use, he never the less had to forage for firewood, pile it and successfully get the flame started. Videos show him munching on a stack of lightly toasted marshmallows.

Many contend that the simple acts performed by the chimps and apes in these experiments are merely a sophisticated form of conditioning. Nevertheless, what about us? We do not come out of the womb acting human. Our ability to interact with society and by societal norms, as seen in feral children, is acquired. We are not born with an innate knowledge of how to navigate the world. We are taught to tie our shoes, cook a meal and even play the violin. We begin by mimicking those around us until we can successfully perform the task ourselves.

The Formation Of Behavior

We have learned a great deal from animals about how learning is shaped and transmitted. Research suggests that our behavior may have formed via two mechanisms. One method of learning is by observing and mimicking others. In this form of education, called *social learning*, skills and behaviors displayed within a group are unintentionally transmitted. Information exchanges are especially prevalent between a parent and her child. The second type behaviors are conditioned behaviors. These are ones that have been imposed upon an individual or a society and then enforced by an external source.

In an experiment performed on the transmission of culture, researcher Gordon Stephenson took eight rhesus monkeys and tested for the transfer of a conditioned response from one monkey to another. Stephenson believed that culture is a constellation of behaviors of a single social group that are learned and then passed on to other members of the group. He looked to prove this with his research.

The monkeys were first paired together into male or female groups. Then a *demonstrator* and the *naïve* subject were identified from each pairing. All of the monkeys were exposed to specific test items to acculturate them to the foreign object. Once acculturated, the demonstrator group were punished with an air blast each time they started to manipulate the test object. The monkeys were blasted several times until they exhibited an avoidance behavior.

When both the demonstrator and naïve subjects were placed in the enclosure with a conditioned object, the demonstrator monkeys displayed threatening facial expressions while being poised in a fear posture. In one group of males, the demonstrator monkey, being placed in the enclosure with the item, moved as far away from the conditioned article as possible. When the naïve monkey was introduced into the pen, it proceeded to the test object without hesitation. When he reached out for the conditioned item, the demonstrator monkey came from the far end of the apparatus, grabbed the other monkey by its flanks and pulled him away. In the 14 remaining minutes of the controlled session, the naïve monkey approached the item several times but never touched it again.

A second research project, performed by primatologists Satsue Mito, offers insights into how learned information can be passed on from one generation to another. It was a hot September day in 1953 when Satsue Mito observed a young female Japanese macaque monkey wash a sweet potato in a small stream. How or where the monkey learned this behavior is unknown. Observations, over the course of years, revealed that the practice of sweet potato washing had spread throughout the troop.

By 1956, females and juveniles exhibited this learned behavior. Monkeys born after 1959 accepted the action as customary and incorporated into their lives without question or resistance. Sixty years and eight generations later, this troop of wild monkeys still practices sweet potato washing.

Did we learn to act human because, like the sign-language monkeys, we took on the behaviors of the gods? Was this newfound knowledge then passed on to our children? Alternatively, were we like Stephenson's rhesus monkeys, conditioned to perform a task or avoid a behavior?

Studies indicate that culture, the fabric of who and what we are, are a learned behavior and not based on biology or instinct. Who was the first to receive an education?

Chapter 5: From Ape to Man

Australopithecines or perhaps *Kenyntropus Platyops*? Were these early hominids, like Pan-banisha and Kanz from the Stone Age Research Center, trained in the manufacture of primitive tools? It does seem curious that not much after we were able to walk upright we somehow figured out how to make tools via the flaking process. The next logical question in our exploration of the human experiences is when did this education begin?

Chapter 6:
A Cognitive Shift

Forms of artistic expression, ritual, and language are universal elements of all known cultures and are exclusively tied to human lineages, including Neanderthals. Contemporary researchers are at a loss when trying to explain the origin of these symbolic practices. Many have come to realize they are not part of our biological inheritance yet are unable to understand the social circumstances that brought about these critical changes amongst prehistoric man.

Language

Why is it that only humans can utilize the complex behavior of language? Our ability to verbalize, biologically speaking, is facilitated by a variety of physiological changes. We are better able to control the passage of air through the mouth and throat because, unlike other animals, our larynx is set low. The location of the hyoid bone in the throat allows for

Chapter 6: A Cognitive Shift

a broader range of tongue, pharyngeal, and laryngeal movements enabling us to make a multitude of distinct speech sounds. Our larger prefrontal cortex gives us the ability to process sentence-level syntax and the capacity to use abstract reasoning including the use of symbols.

Changes also occurred in the FOXP2 gene - the gene known to be directly related to language. Research into human genetics suggests that alterations to this gene in the human lineage evolved recently and rapidly and occurred only with the evolution of our species at most 200,000 years ago. Recent studies into the DNA of *Neanderthals* and *Denisovans* show that they too possessed the modern form of the FOXP2 gene, albeit slightly different. These finds push back the date for when this genetic upgrade was introduced. It also causes us to reevaluate when we, and potentially our nearest cousins were able to utilize language.

Data indicates that *Homo sapiens* and *Neanderthals* split between 465,000 and 569,000 years ago from our last common ancestor *Homo heidelbergensis*. Extrapolating this out just a bit, since *Homo sapiens*, *Neanderthals*, and *Denisovans* all possess this gene, did we ultimately inherit it from *Homo heidelbergensis*? We do not have the genetic data to know one way or the other at this time. It is assumed, however, that there must have been a substantial evolutionary advantage associated with the modern form of the FOXP2 gene. Geneticists also find it hard to understand how the mutation spread so quickly and comprehensively through the population. We will address this concern shortly.

Alec MacAndrew, in his article FOXP2 and the Evolution of Language, states, *"So, in 75 million years since the divergence of mouse and chimpanzee lineages only one change has occurred in FOXP2, (and that equates to 150 million years of evolution as we don't know whether the mutation occurred in the mouse or the primate lineage) whilst in the six million years since the divergence of man and chimpanzee lineages two changes have occurred in the human lineage."*

These physiological changes do not explain how we acquired language. Language is a learned ability. Children who are not exposed to the constructs of human language (feral children) will not pick up language at all. Young children, through trial and error, slowly figure out how to enunciate words correctly and apply the many rules associated with word usage and sentence structure.

Language, conversely, cannot occur unless items in our world have words or names associated with them. How can we call a tree a tree unless there is a word for it? Words allow us to create mental images, which in turn let us recreate our experiences. A mental image, according to *Wikipedia*, is the "*representation in a person's mind of the physical world outside of that person. It is an experience that, on most occasions, significantly resembles the experience of perceiving some object, event, or scene, but occurs when the relevant object, event, or scene is not actually present to the senses.*" Without them, we would be unable to communicate concepts such as "*I saw a deer in the pasture*" or "*I was bitten by a snake*" effectively (Fig. 30).

Figure 30 - Deer in the pasture.

Language is formed by consensus within a community. It does not work if one person wants to call a lion a lion and another a *wurblet*. We encounter this phenomenon when we interact with people who do not speak our language. Where we might say "*Good morning, how are you?*" the same concept would be communicated in China as "*Zǎoshang hǎo nǐ hǎo ma.*" Its meaning, although the same, would be lost because we do not have the vocabulary to transform these words into useful mental images or experiences.

Researchers into the development of language by and large agree that many of today's modern languages would have

Chapter 6: A Cognitive Shift

been too complicated for primitive man to duplicate, but there are a few surviving languages that are believed to be less challenging to vocalize. One language system, the *Khoisan* language system, incorporates a mixture of words, tongue clicks, whistling sounds, and replications of animal and birdcalls, in combination with physical gestures and body language. It is used by several distinct Khoi and San cultural groups in Sub-Sharan Africa but was once spoken all across southern Africa. The Khoisan language does not belong to any other language family on Earth and is believed to be one of the most ancient human tongues, having been spoken for at least, 80,000 years.

Similar to Khoisan is a language used by Lardil people from the Wellesley Islands of Queensland in northern Australia. Called *Damin*, this ancient language also incorporates click consonants and according to indigenous researcher Evan Strong, physical gestures in their vocabulary. Today Damin is a ritual language spoken exclusively by second level initiates and is the only known existent language that uses click sounds outside of Africa. Scholars propose that Damin is a made-up language, but the Lardil people claim that it was created by an ancestral figure known as Kaltharr during the *Alcheringa,* a word used by the Arunta tribe of Australia to describe events that occurred in their far distant past when the gods walked the Earth - the *Dreamtime.*

Linguists have also speculated that in recorded history a third click language existed and was spoken by the indigenous peoples of the Tierra del Fuego Islands of South America. In a letter written by Charles Darwin and recorded in his *The Voyage of the Beagle,* he states: *"The language of these people, according to our notions, scarcely deserves to be called articulate. Captain Cook has compared it to a man clearing his throat, but certainly no European ever cleared his throat with so many hoarse, guttural, and clicking sounds."* Unfortunately, this language has not survived into modern times and this reference is the only documentation of this traditional regional tongue.

The common thread between each of these three click-based languages is that they are all associated with ancient human populations.

If language is a learned skill, who developed it? Who was the first to speak in which the rest of us started emulating? Myth suggests that there was a time when things did not have names. We find this notion reflected in the legends of the Sans people. *"In the beginning,"* according to Bradford Keeney, Ph.D. and Hillary Keeney, Ph.D. in their book *Way Of The Bushman*, *"there were no names. At first, there was no speech. The animals and our original ancestors were happy at the time because they did not have to be concerned about names and differentiating this from that."*

The Bible also recounts a story of giving names to items in our world. *"Out of the ground the LORD God formed every beast of the field and every bird of the sky, and brought them to the man to see what he would call them; and whatever the man called a living creature, that was its name."* - Genesis 2:19. We have a slightly different account in the Quran. Instead of man naming the animals, God teaches Adam their names. *"And He taught Adam the names - all of them."* - Quran 2:31. In South America, the god Viracocha provides names for the world's plants and animals.

Could these stories, like the story of how humanity received an education, reflect the origins of language? Did the abstract concepts associated with verbal communication come from the gods? Were we trained to construct words and sentences so that we could communicate with the divine? Were changes made to our genetic code to improve this ability? Did it allow us to communicate with each other and the gods more efficiently? Language and our ability to use words suggest something else. It infers the ability to create and utilize abstract concepts - a skill only applied to modern man.

Chapter 6: A Cognitive Shift

Art

Like language, figurative art requires abstract reasoning. Art incorporates visual elements with complex meanings attached to them. Art is made up of a series of symbols that can be understood, interpreted and potentially shared with others. It is a library of visual cues. Today, when we see specific images, we can readily recognize the individuals involved, the story being told or the message offered. If we see a picture of Saint Nick, we know intimate details of his life. We can also bring forward vast amounts of information if we observe the representation of a man or woman posted on a door (Fig. 31), come upon a red light as we drive or see a set of golden arches. Without a word spoken, we can understand what it represents and recollect any rules or requirements associated with it.

Figure 31 - Americans With Disabilities Act restroom sign.

This system of communication breaks down if we lose the decoding key. In India, for example, individuals of historical or religious significance are often portrayed with specific attributes including a system of symbolic hand gestures called *Mudras* (Fig. 32). These slight changes to the position of the hand imbue the artwork with subtle meaning and are seen fixed and virtually unchanged throughout the different styles and periods of Indian art. Mudras are used to portray the intent of the individual

Figure 32 - Mudra hand gesture.

65

depicted. They add color and depth to the narrative scenes represented. Some mudras correspond to intentions such as protection, peace, benevolence and dispelling of fear while others signify concepts such as meditation, charity, giving, compassion or knowledge. These seemingly insignificant clues, while their meaning has been preserved in the east, are lost in western consciousness.

Going back in time, the oldest pieces of suggestive art discovered to date are two 77,000-year-old ochre blocks that were found in the *Blombos* cave in South Africa. The artifacts display an etched pattern of overlapping, parallel lines and triangular markings (Fig. 33). Thirteen other pieces of ochre, with inscribed lines on them, have also been found at the same site. Remarkably, Blombos cave has yielded a vast array of incredible finds. Finely carved and decorated bone tools. Beads made from pierced shells. There is also evidence that the cave's residents had meticulously ground ochre into a fine powder and made into a paste. The paste, which could have been used to paint their bodies or faces, was stored in abalone shells, the earliest known containers.

Figure 33 - 77,000 year old ochre block found in Blombos Cave, South Africa.

For years, the simple markings found on these pieces of ochre were surrounded by controversy. Scientists referred to them as *"nothing but random scratching."* Recent finds have caused these modest carvings to be reconsidered and given the place they are due - as the first artistic representations in the world. In another cave in South Africa, called the *Diepkloof Rock Shelter*, Pierre-Jean Texier of the University of Bordeaux and his team has unearthed a cache of ostrich eggshells. Of the 270 fragments discovered, most of the shells were engraved with one of two specific geometric patterns. The 65,000 -

Chapter 6: A Cognitive Shift

55,000-year-old find at Diepkloof is the first archaeological sampling extensive enough to show that our ancestors created design traditions and utilized iconic motifs.

Decorative etched lines, similar to these, have been found on a variety of stones, bones, and shells in ancient sites around the world (Fig. 34). No one knows the meaning of the marks, but like our current iconographic lexicon, could these simple markings represent complex concepts? Were members of the community able to decipher and understand their implicit meaning? It seems obvious that the significance of these symbols, like the mudras of the east, have been lost to the modern eye.

Figure 34 - Engraved sacred stone of Australian First People.
Image courtesy of Even Strong.

A discovery made in 2014 in Java, Indonesia, may actually be the oldest known geometric carving made by a human ancestor. Engraved on a shell that dates to between 540,000 and 430,000 years ago, this ancient artwork was the handicraft of *Homo erectus*. This find is at least four times older than the geometric carvings uncovered in South Africa's Blombos Cave. *"This is the first time we have found evidence for Homo erectus behaving this way. It puts these large bivalve shells and the tools used to engrave them, into the hands of Homo erectus, and will change the way we think about this early human species."* Stephen Munro from School of Archaeology and Anthropology at the Australian National University in Canberra stated.

In another recent find that is making us rethink our history is the discovery of a handful of simple seashells (Fig. 35). The site of Skhul in Israel was initially excavated in the 1930's. In it were three seashells that had a hole pierced in them. The Skhul site dates to at least 100,000 years ago. It is not until recently that the importance of these shells has come to light. They have been identified as the earliest known items of personal adornment discovered, pushing this back the date by almost 25,000 years. *"This study refutes the hypothesis that humans only became culturally modern when they entered Europe 40,000 years ago and replaced Neanderthals"*, says Marian Vanhaeren of University College London, UK.

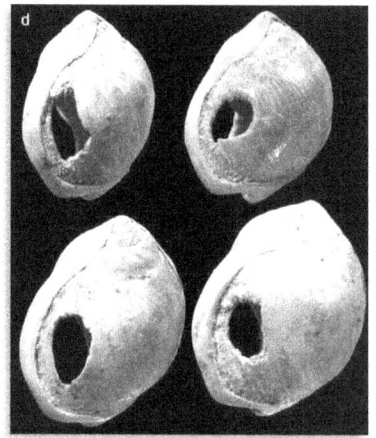

Figure 35 - Pierced shells. Image courtesy of Chris Henshilwood.

The use of jewelry suggests a complex social system. It also shows that our ancestors adopted symbolic behavior much earlier than previously thought. Chris Stringer, an anthropologist at the Natural History Museum in London, noted, *"What we find in Europe is very spectacular. The painted caves are very special, and we've found nothing like them yet in Africa or Asia, but we now know that the basic framework for that behavior was already present around 100,000 years ago."* Researchers are now revisiting the notion that other forms of symbolic material, such as wooden beads or bark paintings, may have existed before 100,000 years ago and has just not survived.

An ability to communicate with one another, be it verbally or through artistic expression, implies something more. It suggests that we had long-lasting and intimate relationships with one another and interacted with social groups whether they are familial or external social ties. Social groups offer us a sense of identity, belonging and safety. We share things in common. Living in a group environment also requires its

Chapter 6: A Cognitive Shift

members to conform to the norms, values, rules, and regulations established by its members. This principle, as you will see, is applied to all societies both ancient and modern.

Chapter 7:
The Fabric Of Society

If you think about it, everyone on the planet lives by a group of principals that constitute a consistent, universal code of morality. These rules govern and guide the actions of persons, organizations, and governments by establishing standards and maintaining order. From the San Fernando Valley to Timbuktu, the basic rules which humanity governs itself are virtually unchanged regardless of which culture and geographic location you explore.

Moral codes dictate right or correct behavior from those that are bad or wrong. They provide a guideline for us to follow - the preverbal *Golden Rule*. Living and interacting with one another, based upon a code of morality, requires that everyone voluntarily submit to the prescribed set of rules and live accordingly. In a perfect world, these

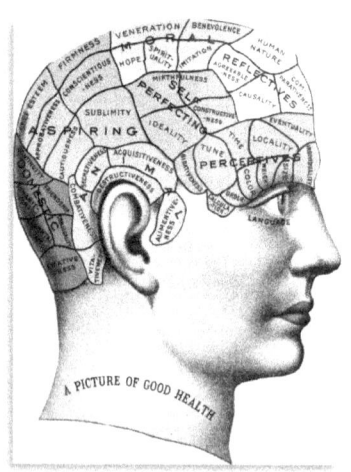

Figure 36 - Turn of the century phrenology map of your mind.

Chapter 7: The Fabric of Society

fundamental principles should ensure that we all live in peace and harmony with one another.

Some speculate that our morality is hardwired into our brains and is deeply rooted in our consciousness (Fig. 36). The principles they offer help to establish the very fabric of society. This conclusion was arrived at because in culture after culture we find a similar group of ethics instituted. Thou shall not kill. Thou shall not steal. Thou shall not commit adultery. If we look to our nearest relatives on the planet, the animal kingdom, do they live by some unspoken code that dictates their behavior?

What if our sense of right and wrong is not an intrinsic part of our genetic make-up as some conjecture? What if it is not an inherent part of the human experience?

Law, according to Wikipedia, is *"a system of rules which are enforced through social institutions to govern behavior."* There are rules that regulate just about everything we do. There are laws that dictate how fast we can drive, whom we can marry and if we can collect the rainwater that falls on our property (rainwater harvesting). State, local and federal agencies mandate secular laws. When not complied with a penalty can and is applied to the offender, the lawbreaker.

Laws create a foundation of what is expected of us. They tell us what to do. They identify the social norm. They are something we do not often think about, yet are pivotal to our ability to be human or to interact with humanity. The amount of control they exert over us is so intense and so ingrained in us that we often do not recognize their implication.

We get a new dog and bring it into our homes. One of our first tasks is to begin housetraining. If the dog complies with our wishes (the law), it is rewarded. If it disregards our commands, it is punished. We, like our new dog, have been taught to comply with a vast set of rules, commandments, and precepts, which we have followed unquestionably over the millennia. If we start stripping away these ordinances, who would we be? Would we still be human? Before we delve into that question, let us create a foundation of our own.

The rules we live by have a long and obscure past. Today we recognize two distinct groups of regulation that control our actions, religious and secular laws, but this was not always the case. The separation of church and state began with the *Age of Enlightenment* and the rise of the sciences. This distinction of laws may have spurred the development of the sciences and helped to launch us into the technological society we have today - but at what cost? This division had one devastating effect. It removed *God* from our lives. It fostered the rise of materialistic thought, which proposes that matter makes up everything in our physical universe and where our entire existence can be explained in material terms.

Many cultures, both ancient and modern, live in a theocracy. In a theocracy, there is no distinction between religious codes and the laws of the state, the laws of God versus the laws of man. Their governing bodies are based on the belief that God is the supreme ruler and his edicts, as dictated by ecclesiastical authorities or a system of priests or holy men, are the laws of the land. Their leader, like the Egyptian God-king, is recognized as the supreme authority and the head of the government.

Thus in the seventieth century when the findings of astronomers such as Galileo and Copernicus went against traditional religious doctrines their discoveries were considered heretical. Since religious law was also secular law, atrocities against the church (or the Pope's opinion) were deemed crimes against the state. In the case of Galileo, he was found guilty of heresy. He was forced to renounce his belief that the Sun was at the center of the solar system and was exiled to Siena. Copernicus, fearing retribution, did not publish his findings until just before his death in 1543.

The origin of our legal system was thought to derive from the *Bible* and the story of Moses and the 10 Commandments. Findings have revealed that the laws dictated to Moses in this ancient account were not the first set of legal decrees instituted.

Chapter 7: The Fabric of Society

Discovered in 1901 by French Egyptologist Gustave Jequier, a code enacted by King Hammurabi in 1772 BC is the most well preserved written ancient system of regulations in existence. It consists of 282 laws that cover criminal matters, contracts, sales and other financial transactions, liability, inheritance, divorce, wages, paternity and sexual behavior. Scaled punishments were associated with the breaking of these laws and were based on an individual's position in their tiered social structure. After its discovery, scholars claimed that the *Code of Hammurabi* was the first set of laws ratified, predating the biblical narrative by some 300 years (Fig. 37). The laws decreed by Moses are reminiscent of the edicts detailed by Hammurabi leading some to speculate that Moses used them as a foundation for his work.

Figure 37 - Stele of Code of Hammurabi.

The establishment date of our legal system changed again in 1952 when an earlier law codex, the *Code of Ur-Nammu*, was unearthed in Nippur. Today, only fragments have been found. This codex dates back to about 2050 BC. The portions of the Code of Ur-Nammu that have survived consist of a preamble and 40 paragraphs which deal primarily with civil and criminal concerns. It seems clear that Hammurabi was familiar with and utilized this text in the formation of his legal system. The language, wording, and punishments sited by Hammurabi are reminiscent of this early exemplar. It appears that, like Moses, many of statutes notated in this previous work were modified and used by Hammurabi.

Texts from the region also indicate that an even earlier system of laws had been in use in Sumer. Called the *Code of Urukagina of Lagash*, this codex predated the Code of Ur-Nammu. We know of the Code of Urukagina because of references to it in other writings. To date, we have yet to recover any tablets of this ancient codex.

What we know about the legal system in Sumner, Babylon, and Assyria is not only derived from these carvings. Legal documents constitute the most substantial number of textual artifacts we have inherited from these Middle Eastern cultures. One of the most extraordinary collections of ancient texts to emerge from this region is associated with King Ashurbanipal (668 – 627BC). Approximately 30,000 stone/clay tablets have been recovered from his palace library. The majority of his collection includes legislative, declarations, contracts, binding agreements, legal decisions, and matters of business and finance. Several other pools of early legal documents have been found in Babylonian temples. These also contribute to our knowledge of early legal systems and their body of laws.

Figure 38 - Sumerian Bill of Sale.
Image courtesy of Marie-Lan Nguyen.

Documents from the earliest periods of Sumerian history until about 2300 BC are minimal. Based on later writing traditions it appears as if by 2300 BC the Sumerian system of laws, rules, and regulations were well developed. Words in their original Sumerian form (cuneiform) were regularly inserted into later Semitic, Babylonian and Assyrian documents. We find a parallel use of Latin terms in today's legal system. Words such as *habeas corpus, ex parte* and *in absentia* are only a few Latin

Chapter 7: The Fabric of Society

words that still appear in our current legal documents. From this convention, we can ascertain that concepts expressed by the inserted Sumerian words were well known and understood in their time.

Ancient Sumerian documents were written on a small rectangular pillow shaped clay tablets (Fig. 38). The tablets were encased in an envelope also made of clay, and both the document and its outer enclosure were marked with a cylinder seal and baked hard. They were literally sealed for posterity. Multiple copies of specific deeds, agreements, and legal outcomes have been discovered. Researchers speculate that the documents were duplicated, with a copy of the decree being given to each of the participants and one copy being placed *on file* at the temple. The decisions recorded would be considered simple in comparison to today's legal mumbo-jumbo, yet the declarations, contracts, and agreements documented on these clay tablets are written in a way that would hold up in any modern court of law.

No concrete evidence of a system of laws predates the Code of Urukagina. It was the dawn of civilization. It was also a time that writing (another gift of the gods) appeared. Writing gave us the opportunity to document our thoughts and ideas, our history and accomplishments. It also provided us with the means to write down our rules and regulations.

Archeologists and other writers of ancient history leave us with the feeling that we were primitive in our thoughts and deeds before the rise of civilization. We cannot assume, based upon a lack of written evidence that no legal, ethical or moral codes existed before to this time. Claude Hermann Walter Johns, in his book *Babylonian and Assyrian Laws, Contracts and Letters* states, *"As far back as we can trace the history or its written monuments there is no time of which we can say, "As yet there is no law.""*

What if we could get an idea of what life was like before the advent of civilization. What did our ancestors hold true? What did they believe in, fear or revere? How did they set their moral compass? The beliefs and societal norms displayed by traditional cultures around the world parallel many of the ones we still hold dear today. These similarities suggest, like our mythic record, that our core values, the fabric of who we are, derived from a singular source and a singular set of ideas. Although a multitude of names describe the embodiment of law, rules, and regulations that controlled these groups, one easily recognizable word that captures the indigenous concept of social control is *taboo*.

Many things in today's social climate are seen as being aberrant and are deemed taboo. Worldwide, there are rules prohibiting sexual intercourse (incest) between different degrees of kinship. Cannibalism, or the practice of consuming human flesh, is considered sacrilegious (Fig. 39). The same holds true for necrophilia, the sleeping or having sexual relations with a dead person. It has only been in very recent times that our view towards inter-racial, inter-religious or homosexual unions has changed, moving them from being taboo to possessing varying levels of social acceptability.

Taboo (tabu/tapu) is a Polynesian word that refers to a person, place or thing that is prohibited or banned. Something can be considered *too sacred* or *too accursed* that it is excluded, separated or

Figure 39 - Indigenous tribe participating in ritual cannibalism.

forbidden. A vast number of items were banned in antiquity. A god or other supernatural being was inherently taboo. So was blood. Coming in contact with a dead body was undoubtedly forbidden as was eating certain kinds of foods. The consequence of interacting with a forbidden item was the threat of supernatural punishment.

Taboos function in a society in much the same way our modern laws do. Dr. Sam Vaknin, in his book *Issues in Ethics*,

Chapter 7: The Fabric of Society

tells us: *"Taboos are pragmatic moral principles. They derive their validity from their efficacy. They are observed because they work, because they yield solutions and provide results."*

The concept of prohibited items is not limited to Polynesia but instead is universal. It is only in our current society that the implication of the word taboo has changed. The deeply held belief in divine intervention and retribution associated with something illicit has been abandoned. We use the word taboo in contemporary vernacular to identify something that is deemed improper, unacceptable or objectionable by society in general. Other than social scorn, the penalties previously tied to something forbidden are no longer applied.

Taboos ruled the lives of our predecessors. Belief in their power was commanding. There was a mysterious and dangerous quality to them. A person, who was exposed to something that was prohibited, was perceived as being infected. The infection they carried was communicable and life-threatening. The taboo, like a rampant virus, would infect anyone the contagious individual encountered. Instead of worrying about the aches and pains of a physical malady, they dreaded the retribution of the gods for transgressing a divine command. Stories have emerged of individuals getting sick and dying after being infected by this powerful charm. These stories further supported the power taboos held over a community.

Figure 40 - Sigmund Freud, circa 1926.

The rules, regulations, customs, and traditions held by ancient and indigenous groups may seem strange to us, but the concepts expressed underlie the values and morals of modern society and many of today's religions. They created structure in their lives and allow them to interact in larger social groups. They let its members know, akin to our modern legal system, what was expected of them as well as what the penalty was for non-compliance.

Sigmund Freud (Fig. 40) in his book *Totem & Taboo* notes, "*Taboos are very ancient prohibitions which at one time were forced upon a generation of primitive people from without, that is, they probably were forcibly impressed upon them by an earlier generation.*" Who established our laws, taboos and moral codes in the first place? Why dictate our behavior? Who decided what we should value and what we should shun? Myth suggests it was the gods. But, why would they want to? We will be revising this concept again a little later on.

Whatever their reasoning, their purpose continues to be a mystery, and these questions remain unanswered. We can only speculate as to their motives. We can, however, look at ourselves and the overwhelming number of edicts, in the form of beliefs, rules, regulations, taboos, customs, and traditions that we accept and buy into in our daily lives. With that said, one of the oldest and most consistent set of restrictions found on the planet has to do with the concept of marriage.

Love And Marriage

Getting married is an age-old celebration, which commemorates the joining of two individuals together in holy matrimony. For many in today's society, it represents picking out invitations, dresses, decorations, food, and flowers and finally tying the knot. Yet getting married is more than just fun and frivolities. It is a ritualized contract that forms a legal partnership between two individuals. This contract establishes the rights and obligations of the happy couple and those of any potential offspring.

Marriage is heavily steeped in local customs and religious dogma. The institution of marriage, it is believed, found its

Chapter 7: The Fabric of Society

origin in the ancient world as a means of preserving power, forging alliances, acquiring land and producing legitimate heirs. It was a tool used to organize families, and like most other social institutions, this time-honored tradition has evolved over the centuries.

The earliest evidence supporting marriage, and the marriage contract, appears in the Code of Hammurabi. This legal mandate contains 33 specific edicts that establish the rights and obligations of married couples covering topics such as bride-price, divorce, marital debt, incest, and adultery. The well thought out concepts contained in this early text make it clear that the rules and regulations associated with marriage have a much older past.

As we delve into the roots and history of marriage, several noteworthy facts quickly emerge. Early explorers, as they traveled the globe to investigate indigenous cultures, unearthed revealing information regarding marriage. They discovered that even the most remote groups they interacted with had well-defined systems that regulated nuptials as well.

Marriage was ruled by taboos. Two of the longest lasting prohibitions, tied to the happy couple, revolve around the concept of having sex with a married woman (adultery) and having sexual relations with someone from your own clan. Both were expressly forbidden.

Many cultures consider adultery a serious crime. The US military has strict rules of conduct, which include infidelity. Surprisingly, over one-half of the states in the United States still have adultery laws on the books. A fine or even a jail sentence can punish offenders of this seemly-outdated crime.

Adultery was a severe offense in antiquity. In the *Bible*, for example, the sixth commandment states, *"Thou shalt not commit adultery"* and goes on to inform us in the eighth commandment that it is *"forbidden to covet your neighbor's wife."* Individuals caught in these compromising situations would be put to death. If a married woman, according to the *Code of Hammurabi*, is accused of lying with another man, she was prosecuted and drowned as punishment.

We find similar laws and punishments in many indigenous cultures. In Polynesia, it is death to touch the wife of another man. In Zimbabwe, the penalty for adultery is death. Adulterers, in Rome, were banished to an island. An unfaithful wife would have her body mutilated in Native American cultures, while amongst the Aztecs, a common punishment was stoning an individual to death. One standard, although brutal form of punishment for doing the dirty deed was rhinotomy, the amputation of the nose. This disfiguring procedure was practiced amongst the Greeks and Romans, in Arab nations, in India, Egypt and Native Americans populations.

Intriguingly, in many societies, the prescribed laws and associated punishments were dictated for women and less so, if not at all, for men. Men, in many of these cultures, were often given the liberty to have sex with a slave or an unmarried woman. Once a woman married, she became taboo and was off limit.

The second part of the marriage duo, or should I say, **do not**, was to marry or have sexual relations with members of your own clan. This practice was a big no-no.

Each clan was associated with a specific animal, the group's totem (Fig. 41). Many cultures believe that a group's totem animal represented the embodiment of a god on Earth. Believers contend that it was from these divine animals that they owe their descent. It was through the use of totem animals that individuals could recognize their relationship to one another. This association helped them keep this most sacred rule. No one knows how or why the institution and regulations tied to totems and clans came into existence, but the laws that come from this

Figure 41 - Madagascar Lemur.

early practice are rich and complex. Research suggests that even though every culture on earth partakes and relishes the

Chapter 7: The Fabric of Society

holy, consecrated and commemorated union between two individuals, it is believed that the marriage vow preceded many of the laws, customs, and traditions we have today.

There is just one exception to the widespread practice of the marriage taboo, and examples of it are only found in stratified cultures, meaning in cultures that exhibit social classes. In nations with a strong ruling class, such as in South America (Inca), in Egypt and China, it was a common practice to have the god-king marry his sister or half-sister.

Is the impulse to marry part of what it is to be human? Is it an integral part of who we are? Our closest primate relatives do not marry. They are either promiscuous or polygynous. Monogamous pairing does not exist in these groups. Males provide little parental care, leaving the mother solely responsible for infant rearing. D. Lukas and T. H. Clutton-Brock, in their article *The Evolution of Social Monogamy in Mammals*, suggest that social monogamy evolves in mammals when females occupy small and discrete ranges where males cannot monopolize more than one female. Infanticide risk may have also led to close attendance by resident males which in turn increased social monogamy and bi-parental care.

If our compulsion to create permanent and long-term attachments to our mate is not part of our genetic makeup, did **we**, as part of human social evolution, develop societal rules to regulate marriage? If we did, one would expect to find groups with no marriage rules or a helter-skelter set of laws imposed randomly upon individual cultures. Dr. Ashley Montague, a noted British-American anthropologist, stated, *"There are no societies in which marriage does not exist."* He goes on to assert, *"If marriage developed in a random, haphazard, evolutionary fashion, one might expect that "marriage" would be found in some cultures but not in others. The evidence, however, simply did not support that view."* The early systems of marital laws he uncovered were remarkably consistent around the globe, so consistent that early pioneers in the world of anthropology stated that this tradition bears the stamp of *deliberate design.*

C. Owen Lovejoy, an anthropologist at Kent State University in Ohio, writing in the early 1980's, came up with an explanation for not only the origin of marriage but bipedalism as well. He suggested that this unique method of locomotion did not develop because the environment for early hominids had changed from jungle to savanna. Instead, he alleges that walking upright co-evolved with monogamy and possibly marriage. Lovejoy believed that females, in return for food, would mate exclusively with a male who would in-return take care of his babies. Lovejoy reasoned that it was easier to gather food and carry it back to your *family* if your arms were free.

While I do not agree with Mr. Lovejoy's theory of monogamy and marriage could there be at least some merit to his thoughts? It only took a few generations before the entire troop of macaque monkeys in Japan to begin washing sweet potatoes. If a rudimentary form of clanship and nuptials originated as we started to walk upright, what other laws, rules or taboos came into being in these early hominid populations?

If the rules that surround the marriage right did not originate in man's psyche, did the gods create the obligations and conventions associated with it? Marriage was one of the first traditions imposed upon humanity by the gods according to Baldwin Spencer and F.J. Gillen in their book *The Native Tribes of Central Australia*. It came after the rite of circumcision and subincision (topics we will delve into as we progress). The marriage tradition is said to have come from the *Alcheringa,* the Australian Dreamtime. Biblical texts infer that God ordained the laws by which we live, including martial requirements. We find a similar celestial reference when reviewing ancient legal systems like the Code of Hammurabi. If the gods did impose these restrictions on humanity, what was their intention?

Were we, like the formation of corn and modern bread wheat, genetically engineered? If this assertion is correct, what are the implications of this breeding process? First off, if modifications were made to our genetic makeup, as mythology suggests, a group of genetically modified hybrid humans (the

Vanara?) were introduced into existing indigenous populations. If this newly created species of ape-men were allowed to mate randomly, the chances of spreading their updated genetic material could be limited. Did the gods foresee a potential problem? Did they establish a system of rules that would ensure genetic variation?

Ancient marital laws forced individuals to mate with men and women from different groups. This practice would naturally increase the distribution of hybridized genetic materials. This method of gene manipulation (gene flow) would ultimately alter the genetic makeup of an array of diverse populations and if given enough time could affect everyone. In the inverse, it would preserve inherited traits and maintain a pure bloodline as seen in cultures that allow marriage between close familial members.

Was the holy, consecrated and commemorated union between two individuals formulated to organize family groups, forge an alliance or maintain power or was something more divine at work? If the gods imposed the institution of marriage upon us, it does explain the level of consistency, the stamp of *deliberate design*, we see around the world today. As we continue our exploration of the foundation of humanity, we will be examining a series of universal traditions that transcend culture. We can only assume that, like the distribution of marriage rites, these customs are ancient.

Chapter 8:
All Things Sacred

The God-King

A god or other supernatural being was inherently taboo. Their representatives, the god-king or priest, were thought of as an incarnation of god and were endowed with superhuman abilities (Fig. 42). They were the upholder of universal order. If things were in balance, the society prospered, but if the god-king failed, everyone suffered. In this role, he was the source of endless blessings and inestimable danger.

These earthly representatives of the gods had power over nature. The weather was under his control. People thrived if they honored the gods and obeyed his laws. The natural world, on the

Figure 42 - Mesoamerican God-king.

Chapter 8: All Things Sacred

other hand, would be disturbed and catastrophes would occur if there were a lapse in their devotion. The weather could turn causing crops to fail. Calamities or other misfortunes could scourge the land. The power of the god-king was so vast that any neglect on his part could affect the entire world because he alone sustained it.

Great care was required of the god-king. Irreparable damage to the world could occur if he turned his head or lifted his arm a certain way. His actions, both voluntary and involuntary could upset the established order of the universe and unleash every form of evil upon it.

> *The life of the kings of Egypt, says Diodorus, was not like that of other monarchs who are irresponsible and may do just what they choose; on the contrary, everything was fixed for them by law, not only their official duties, but even the details of their daily life... . The hours both of day and night were arranged at which the king had to do, not what he pleased, but what was prescribed for him... . For not only were the times appointed at which he should transact public business or sit in judgment; but the very hours for his walking and bathing and sleeping with his wife, and, in short, performing every act of life were all settled. Custom enjoined a simple diet; the only flesh he might eat was veal and goose, and he might only drink a prescribed quantity of wine.*
>
> – The Golden Bough, James Frazer

A god, or his human counterpart, could not be touched. His power was so immense that even the sun was not worthy to shine upon him. He and all of his possessions were holy and forbidden. If he touched one of his subjects or something that belonged to them, its status changed immediately. If a divinity walked on the ground, the ground became sacred and inaccessible to the common man. Many cultures, to err on the side of caution, would carry the god-king upon a litter, so his feet did not touch the earth.

No one spoke the names of the gods. It was even forbidden in some cultures to look upon a god. Similarly, if he looked at an individual, that person, in fact, anything the god-king's sacred eyes gazed upon was instantly transformed. The affected object was now sacred and could no longer be used by mere mortals. The god-king's dishes, in some cultures, were only used once. These plates and bowls, out of fear that if a layman ate out of these sacred vestals, a malady would occur, were immediately broken. Even his discarded hair and nails were sacrosanct. Once cut, these remnants were burned or buried.

Sacred items were only accessible to a select few. The potential danger associated with coming into contact with a god, or his property, was enormous. Consecrated objects were believed to be extremely powerful, and individuals who interacted with them needed to be adequately strengthened. Priests and holy men who worked with the god-king practiced elaborate rites and rituals before their exposure to these untouchable items. In some cultures, unique garments were worn that were reserved for this purpose. These additional precautions prepared these individuals for their interaction with the divine (Fig.43).

Figure 43 - Jewish priest Aaron wearing specialized garments.

Pomp and circumstance did not fill the god-king's life. It overflowed with a myriad of prohibitions, rites, rituals, and ceremonies. These observances, while intending to preserve harmony within the universe, restrained his every act and took away his freedom. The god-king's life was many times filled with sorrow and considered a burden. The homage and devotion lavished on him could come to an abrupt ended if tragedy struck. He could be worshiped as a god one day and just as quickly be killed the next to make room for someone who could preserve their world.

Countless prohibitions also surrounded an heir to the throne. They would accumulate as he grew from childhood and would often suffocate him by the time he was crowned. In some cultures, the man who was chosen to be a group's leader was taken into custody until he relented and became willing to take on the role. The restrictions associated with the office were so overwhelming that in several societies the job of king was given to complete strangers.

Divine Fluid

Blood, as a divine fluid and the essence of life, was also inherently sacred. It, like the god-king, was not to be touched. Anything that blood fell upon was rendered taboo making it unusable for everyday purposes. This interdiction included human blood as well as animal blood. The blood of a kinsman or the group's totem animal was especially hallowed. Prohibitions around the sanctity of blood extended to the individual who shed the blood. He or she would become immediately tainted after a kill or contact.

Animals were not hunted, caught, and killed in the irreverent way they are today. There was a deep respect for the animal and its role in their lives. Rituals and observances were performed before the hunt. Ceremonies and songs would thank the animal spirit, after it was killed, for giving its life. This reverence also extended during the butchering process. Throughout, the gods and the spirit of the animal were praised for being willing to participate in their success.

Warriors, who shed the blood of their enemies, also fell under the blood prohibition. Victorious warriors, like the successful hunters, offered sacrifices on behalf of their adversaries. They would mourn their fallen enemies. A song would be sung in their honor, a prayer said, all to implore their forgiveness with the hope that they will rest in peace.

Figure 44 - Indian Toda Hut.
Image courtesy of Pratheepps.

A man, after killing an animal or an enemy was prohibited from interacting with society and would enter into a period of purification to remove their tabooed status. Touching an impure man during this interval, an item he touched, sat or laid upon would contaminate the other person. They remained in this state until a prescribed time had elapsed, which could last for a few days to several months depending on the tradition. Huts were erected on the outskirts of the village for them to stay in during their purification phase (Fig. 44).

Contact with a woman, during their menstrual period, was also prohibited. Like the men in the community, women would pass their time in special shelters thus helping to avoid any accidental contact. Sinu Joseph in her article *Menstrual Taboos and Ancient Wisdom* informs us:

> *Menstruating women were considered to be having special powers during menstruation, which if not used properly could cause harm to others. In addition, practical reasons of predatory animals smelling the blood in ancient times and coming for the kill, would have led to these women being kept in separate huts to protect the community. Since most ancestral women menstruated at the same time with the new moon, the seclusion huts (also called moon huts) were filled with*

women with special powers who together performed sacred rituals for the good of the community. Women who came out of the seclusion hut were revered for their visions and wisdom gained during this time, and often guided the community as to where to go for hunting, etc.

– Menstrual Taboos and Ancient Wisdom, Sinu Joseph

A handful of researchers believe that a woman during her cycle was initially envisioned as being sacred and not *unclean* as we find in contemporary culture. We can only conclude that the sacredness of women and menstrual blood changed from being a divine fluid to being viewed as undesirable when societies shifted from matriarchal to patriarchal lineages. This shift is thought to have occurred somewhere around 10,000 BC. The prohibition against contact with a woman during this time, took a harsh tone in some cultures as is reflected in the Old Testament book of Leviticus section 15:19 - 30

19 And if a woman have an issue, and her issue in her flesh be blood, she shall be put apart seven days: and whosoever toucheth her shall be unclean until the even.

20 And every thing that she lieth upon in her separation shall be unclean: every thing also that she sitteth upon shall be unclean.

21 And whosoever toucheth her bed shall wash his clothes, and bathe himself in water, and be unclean until the even.

22 And whosoever toucheth any thing that she sat upon shall wash his clothes, and bathe himself in water, and be unclean until the even.

23 And if it be on her bed, or on any thing whereon she sitteth, when he toucheth it, he shall be unclean until the even.

24 And if any man lie with her at all, and her flowers be upon him, he shall be unclean seven days; and all the bed whereon he lieth shall be unclean.

25 And if a woman have an issue of her blood many days out of the time of her separation, or if it run beyond the time of her separation; all the days of the issue of her uncleanness shall be as the days of her separation: she shall be unclean.

26 Every bed whereon she lieth all the days of her issue shall be unto her as the bed of her separation: and whatsoever she sitteth upon shall be unclean, as the uncleanness of her separation.

27 And whosoever toucheth those things shall be unclean, and shall wash his clothes, and bathe himself in water, and be unclean until the even.

28 But if she be cleansed of her issue, then she shall number to herself seven days, and after that she shall be clean.

29 And on the eighth day she shall take unto her two turtles, or two young pigeons, and bring them unto the priest, to the door of the tabernacle of the congregation.

30 And the priest shall offer the one for a sin offering, and the other for a burnt offering; and the priest shall make an atonement for her before the LORD for the issue of her uncleanness.

– Leviticus 15:19 - 30

As a woman, all I can say is ouch!

The same prohibition held true for newborn babies and their mothers. They were barred from interacting with society until a prescribed time had elapsed. Rituals, such as the sprinkling of water on the child's head or the emersion in water, purified the child allowing him or her to join the community at large. A form of this cleansing ritual is still being implemented in many contemporary cultures and amongst modern day Christians.

Contact With The Dead

An assortment of interesting things occurred when someone died. The house the deceased live in, in some cultures, was torn down, burned with all of his or her possessions inside or were deserted, never to be used again. Many cultures avoided saying the name of the newly departed. If spoken, a severe penalty was imposed. In some groups, it was customary to change the deceased name so that it could be spoken without fear of retribution. Even the reliving of fond memories of the individual, something we frequently do when a loved one has died, was also prohibited.

Interacting with a dead body was also barred. It rendered the mourners and anyone else who came in contact with the departed individual unclean, thus taboo. Once the period of segregation was over, the person could again mingle with his fellow beings. Items used during this time were burned, buried or somehow destroyed. The dishes used by mourners were often broken to preclude reuse. They threw away the clothes they wore. Many shaved their heads, prepared their nails and put on clean clothing to indicate that their mourning period was over.

Ritual Purification & Rebirth

Ones tabooed status could only be lifted through the use of cleansing and purification. Ritual purification was used to remove specifically defined *uncleanliness* and reestablish one's purity. All known cultures and religions practice this ceremonial act, both ancient and modern. Ritual purification can take many different forms. Some involve performing one or two simple gestures, such as reciting a prayer while others include ordeals including bloodletting, animal sacrifice or beating to have a purgative effect.

The most common tool used to cleanse oneself ritually is water. Its use in eliminating ones unclean or improper status is widespread. A person might wash their whole body or only certain parts of it like their hands or feet. Water may be sprinkled, thrown, poured, or blown upon a person or object to cleanse it. It could take the form of entering a sacred river and immersing themselves, or by having the group's priest, holy man or shaman sprinkle water on them using the bough of a sacred tree.

Many societies utilized sweat baths or steam baths to remove impurities. Native American, Mexican, Guatemalan, Asian, African, Finnish and Indian cultures all employ this practice. The oldest known record of a sweat bath appears in the Sanskrit treatise *The Ayurveda*, thought to have been written in 568 BC. This ancient medical text identifies thirteen methods of inducing sweat in the body, including the use of the sweat bath. In Native American cultures, this purification ceremony is commonly referred to as a sweat lodge. This ritual aims to purify one's mind, body, spirit, and heart and was considered to be a process of rebirth and renewal. Similarly, a sauna (sweat bath) was taken before any significant feast or festival to cleanse and purify the individual in Finland.

Fire, in many indigenous cultures, also acts as a powerful transformer. Its cleansing action supports the renewal of the human spirit. The ancient practice of firewalking as a means of purification shares a worldwide distribution like the use of

Chapter 8: All Things Sacred

water as a cleansing tool (Fig. 45). Firewalking takes several forms. Individuals in need of cleansing may be required to walk around or jump over a fire. The most common kind of firewalking involves an individual walking briskly over a layer of hot coals that are thinly spread out along the ground or on the bottom of a shallow channel.

Figure 45 - Fire walking.
Image courtesy of Roxana Coach.

Where this observance began is unknown, but according to some researchers, it is believed to have originated in Africa over 4000 years ago. Some claim that the earliest known reference to it comes from Central Asia. The most definitive testimonial to firewalking comes from ancient Rome. Author, Pliny the Elder tells us, *"at the yearly sacrifice to Apollo, performed on Mount Soracte, walk over a charred pile of logs without being scorched and who consequently, under a perpetual decree of the Senate, enjoy exemption from military service and all other burdens."* Other ancient writers including Strabo and Virgil recorded this annual event. Mentions of it also appear in the *Bible*. *"Can one go upon hot coals, and his feet not be burned?"* - Proverbs 6:28 and *"When thou walkest through the fire, thou shalt not be burned"* - Isaiah 43:2 are two well-known examples.

Firewalking was a serious affair. Participants would prepare themselves for the ordeal by cleansing, fasting, meditating, praying, chanting, and ritual dancing. In some cultures, participants could not speak to a woman, smoke, drink or have sexual intercourse before the trial. The length of these rights varied by culture and could last for several days or until the person was sufficiently *charged*, a sign that they were prepared to begin this challenge.

Related to the use of fire for ritual purification is the employing of smoke to cleanse polluted items. This powerful ancient technique has been used to drive away negative energies and restore balance to individuals, spaces, and things. Indigenous people around the world have utilized the beneficial properties that smoke offers for thousands of years. Evidence for its uses has been found globally and would take the form of the burning of aromatic woods, herbs, and leaves (incense).

The widespread use of incense in purification rites finds its roots in the transformative power of fire, as well as on the additional benefits associated with the sweet smells and their associated therapeutic use. Items in need of cleansing may be singed, fumigated, or smoked. Incense was also used in rituals to deepen meditation and provide a connection between the physical and spiritual worlds where contact with the divine could be achieved through its smoke.

The practice of using smoke for inner cleansing has only come into Western consciousness recently. We have learned of it from the Amerindian culture where it is called *smudging*. Smudging (the name given to the sacred smoke bowl blessing) has been a part of Native American tradition since ancient times. It was used to cleanse themselves before a holy ceremony or before calling on the spirits.

One of the earliest records of smoke being used as part of a ritual comes from ancient Egypt. They believed that the smoke and fragrance of the incense embodied their deities. On a tablet found in Giza, Egypt, dating to about 1530 BC, indicates that as part of their religious ceremonies herbs were being burned. The use of incense also appears in the Old Testament of the Bible where God commands Aaron to burn sweet spices on the altar. *"And Aaron shall burn thereon incense of sweet spices; every morning, when he dresseth the lamps, he shall burn it."* - Exodus 30:7. The practice of burning incense or smoke cleansing is still practiced in every dominant religion on the globe today (Fig. 46).

Chapter 8: All Things Sacred

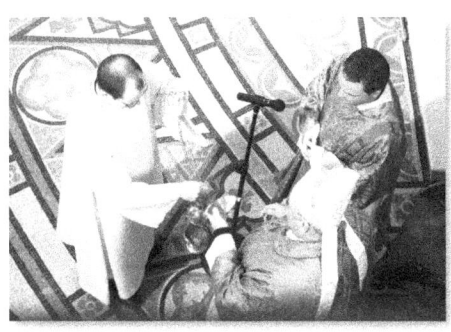

Figure 46 - Catholic priest burning incense as Mass.

The rules that govern tabooed items in antiquity, whether it is the god-king, contact with blood or the dead are clear and consistent regardless of where one looks. The same holds true with the guidelines that surround ritual cleansing in its various forms. Again, questions remain. Why were these items deemed off limit?

Did the gods, in our far distant past, spend time on the Earth? Was physical contact with these otherworldly beings, for whatever reason, expressly forbidden? Over time, did the rulership of the Earth get handed off to their semidivine counterparts, the demigods, such as the Greek Hercules and Perseus or the Indian Vanara, that dot myth? Was this convention ingrained in our psyches? Even in the present day, a king is habitually thought of as a god on Earth, but why?

Then there is the whole notion of taboos. Today, at least on the surface, no ill will or malice has ever affected anyone who comes into contact with human or animal blood or the body of a deceased relative. The sky has not fallen. People are not dropping like flies every time they eat a hamburger. In the same breath, we should not preclude the impact these things may have on deeper levels of our beings. We will come back and address the potential ramifications of taboos on the soul later on.

Chapter 9:
The Invisible World

All religious beliefs and beliefs about the nature of the world, in general, had to have begun somewhere. English anthropologist Edward Burnett Tylor, in his work *Primitive Culture* and *Anthropology*, set the stage for our modern understanding of the underpinnings of religion. He suggested that all religious thought evolved as societies progressed. Tylor believed that as a civilization's technological constructs advanced so did their explanations of natural phenomena. He concluded that monotheism, the belief that there is only one God, was the pinnacle of religious thought and signified an advanced level of development over *primitive* hunter-gatherer cultures.

In our ongoing exploration into the nature of humanity, we find that the most common, foundational thread that underlies all religious and spiritual traditions is that of animism. Animism is the oldest known belief system in the world. It transcends geographical areas and time periods, from Paleolithic Africa to modern North America. It is still a primary component of many indigenous and traditional societies. Even Europe had rich animistic traditions in the past. Ethnologists have concluded that every race and culture on Earth incorporated some form of animism into his or her spiritual beliefs at some time in their history.

Chapter 9: The Invisible World

Animism asserts that the entire universe, and everything in it, is alive, interrelated and filled with energy (Fig. 47). It has a consciousness, a soul. This spirit, this animating spark, is not a trait that is exclusive to humankind but exists in every animal and plant, in non-living objects such as rocks and rivers and natural phenomena such as the weather. If you have ever had the profound internalized feeling that everything is connected and you are just a small part of this giant interconnecting web of life, then you may have glimpsed the world as perceived by animistic practitioners.

Figure 47 - Illustration of the subtle world we live in.

In a more modern vernacular, this same concept states that all things, including man, are made up of an array of interconnecting energies and energetic fields. Over 50 different and distinct terms have been used to describe this energy according to a National Institute of Health study. They include chi, prana, holy spirit, manna, ether, orgone, biomagnetism, and zero-point. While many may think that this is a modern *New Age* concept, Babylonian priests who recognized this underlying, animating principal thousands of years ago called it *zi* or *life*. It appears that many aspects of life in ancient and indigenous cultures revolved around dealing with and interacting with this unseen force.

Tied to the belief that everything in our universe is filled with life force energy is the concept of the existence of souls or spirits who live outside of, yet are part of the natural world. God, spirit or soul, these non-corporeal beings were an intimate part of indigenous life and helped form the basis of their religious beliefs. These spirits are thought to guide individuals through life. They acted as teachers and in some instances, protected them from evil. These disembodied souls, according to many cultures, were not always kind and loving but were envisioned as malevolent demons that torment the living. It is this, the idea of non-corporeal spirits inhabiting our world, which we will be exploring first.

Manes, Lemures, and Larvae

Regardless of where they looked, individuals saw the world swarming with invisible spirits of their dearly departed. The fear of interacting with one of these lost souls dominated their thoughts and actions. This concept may seem strange to us in contemporary western society, but the belief in the existence of ethereal spirits is still held by us today. Nowadays we call these phantom presences *ghosts*.

The notion of ghostly spirits roaming the Earth holds an unusual place in our thoughts. These invisible beings have been described as plaguing humanity in our earliest known texts and are still being reported today. One thing that ghosts and the gods of myth have in common is that they are both invisible to the naked eye. Contemporary scholars allege that they are both a byproduct of someone's wild imagination that is unless discussions revolve around the one true creator God of the West.

Ghosts, unlike the gods, were not represented on cave walls, on funerary monuments or pottery. They were not worshiped or prayed to. Their lives do not figure prominently in our mythic history. No epic narrative that features a ghost as the main character exists. These spooky tales of things that go bump in the night are not filled with drama, intrigue, and suspense like those of the gods - unless the author is telling a ghostly yarn. Even when the spirit of the dearly departed is encountered in an ancient mythological tale, they are never

Chapter 9: The Invisible World

portrayed as being real but are always recognized for what they are - an apparition.

Ghosts, from a very early time, have had their detractors and have remained on the cusp of belief. Tales of ghosts, even today, fall into two categories: ghost stories and ghostly encounters. It is by and large accepted that any good ghost story is designed to scare the listener and are recognized as being a fictitious tale (Fig. 48). On the other hand, when someone experiences one of these non-corporeal beings first hand its appearance has been memorialized in much the same way a modern ghost hunter would document a sighting. These disembodied spirits are often described as retaining their original personality but are a vague, unsubstantial, immaterial copy of their former selves. A ghost is genuine to the individual who sees one, but the account of their terrifying incident is often dismissed and not believed by others.

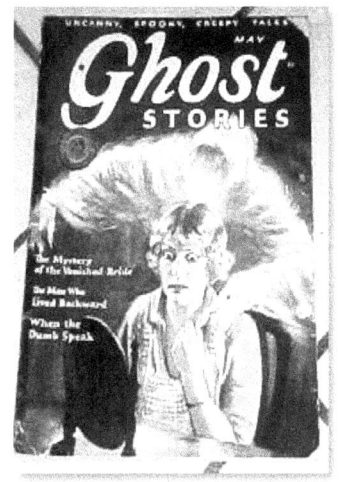

Figure 48 - Cover of Ghost Stories magazine

The faith in life after physical death is ancient. Many cultures understand that when we die, the souls of the lucky ones will ascend into the heavens and live for eternity. The rest of us, sad as it is to say, will reside somewhere within the bowels of the Earth in the gloom of Hades (or the appropriate name provided by the local culture). This underground home of the God of Death was not one of torture and punishment, as is envisioned today, but was a resting place for the soul. And, even though there is an association between death, dying, ghosts and the God of the Underworld, ghosts are never referred to as demons (except in certain Christian beliefs) or as a minion of the God of Death. (ET Chronicles – Who Art In Heaven)

Spirits had three classifications in Rome. They were broken up into *manes, lemures,* and *larvae*. Manes were thought to represent the soul of loved ones who dwell in the underworld. Lemures were vengeful spirits who wandered the earth. These wicked and restless specters haunted the living and caused injury. Associated with the lemures are the larvae. Larvae are apparitions that haunt houses and could scare the bejesus out of you. The Roman grammarian Festus explains that they were *"the shadows of the dead who gave no rest in the house they were in either to the Masters or the servants."* From a present-day perspective of ghostly phenomena, the difference between lemures and larvae is similar to what is currently described as an active verse a residual haunting.

Traditional cultures seem to agree with Festus on one thing when it comes to ghosts. They believed that **IF** the soul of the departed individual is not at rest, it will come back and haunt you. They feared the return of the spirit of the dead. Their overwhelming dread of malicious and malevolent spirits was so great that additional rules, regulations, rituals, taboos, and prohibitions were established which added another level of control in their lives. They believed that these non-corporeal beings walking the earth could be hostile and even dangerous to the living. They could possess you or torture you. They could send plagues, cause illness and in extreme cases even death. They were blamed for most ill fortunes and instances of bad luck that overcame an individual.

The most common reasons given for the inability of a soul to find peace in the hereafter (both in the past and in the present) include: they had to complete a task; they wanted to enact revenge, or they wanted to fulfill a promise. The departed may also return to the mortal world and wander the earth because they died a violent death, committed suicide or as repayment for the evil things they did in life. The most widespread and universal belief associated with the concept of death and dying is: if an individual does not receive a proper burial they will return to the land of the living.

Chapter 9: The Invisible World

If a person was not interred correctly, in ancient Greece, they were not allowed to enter into Hades, the land of the dead. Their spirit was doomed to roam around outside of the underworld where they would haunt the living. In Egypt, if the tomb of a Pharaoh is disturbed, it is believed that its mummified body would find you and torment you for the rest of your life. The Navajo Indians understood that if someone did not receive proper funeral rites, his or her spirit was destined to remain on the earthly plane where it would torture the living. Dogon funerary rites, according to cosmologist Laird Scranton, is to *"reassure this soul that all is well here among the living and to encourage it to move on. Because some souls choose not to move on, ceremonial funerals are periodically held to offer those souls additional chances to do so"*.

Death, mourning, and burial rituals are something we take for granted in today's society. It is what we do when a friend or loved one pass. When compared to any other life form on Earth this behavior is quite unusual, yet this practice was imperative and highly significant in early cultures. Words were spoken over the dead. A song was sung, or a prayer was uttered to help ensure the departed crossed over well. The *Tibetan Book Of The Dead* offers mourners a step-by-step guide of what they can do to ensure the dead will not get trapped on Earth. The steps include reminding the deceased they are dead and that it is time for them to enter *into the light*.

We can only speculate when our belief in ghosts began. The word ghost is a relatively modern one. It entered the English vernacular in the late sixteenth century. It came from the archaic Germanic word *gast* which means to terrify or frighten. The first mention that testifies to our knowledge and understanding of the concept of ghosts appears in the Sumerian *Epic of Gilgamesh*. The earliest known written version of this tale dates back to 2100 BC. It tells the story of the demi-god Gilgamesh and his friend Enkidu (we discussed the education of Enkidu earlier). In a dream, Enkidu discovers that the gods destined his fate – he was going to die.

> *Enkidu was lying (sick) in front of Gilgamesh.*
> *His tears flowing like canals, he (Gilgamesh) said:*
> *"O brother, dear brother, why are they absolving me*
> *instead of my brother"*
> *Then Enkidu said: "So now must I become a ghost,*
> *to sit with the ghosts of the dead, to see my dear brother*
> *nevermore!"*
>
> – Epic of Gilgamesh: Tablet VII

The first-century Roman historian, Pliny the Younger, wrote of a ghost who haunted his home in Athens. In his chronicles, he described an otherworldly vision he had of an old man with a long beard, rattling a chain. Stories of ghostly encounters also appear in the writings of Homer, Vergil, Herodotus, and Plutarch.

The archeological records may suggest that a belief in these non-corporeal beings may go back even further. The deliberate disposal of the dead appears in the archeological record starting around 100,000 years ago with the intentional burial of *Homo neanderthalensis* and *Homo sapiens*. Bodies unearthed have been discovered lying on their side in a flexed position, covered with a red/orange pigment call ochre and interred with grave goods, which included food, tools, and medicinal herbs. Did they, like the relatively recent burial practices of the Egyptians and the Inca, believe that grave goods would help the deceased as they journeyed on into the afterlife (Fig. 49)?

Figure 49 - Ancient burial with grave goods

The prospect of the spirit of the dead returning to the land of the living was always met with apprehension. People were so terrified of this potentiality that they took additional

Chapter 9: The Invisible World

measures to save themselves. In Norse traditions, for example, the big toes were tied together, or needles were driven through the soles of the feet to keep the deceased from walking the earth. In the Mayan culture, individuals were laid to rest with corn in their mouths to provide them with food for their journey to the otherworld. Many Mayan sites also had the entrance of the burial chamber oriented in a way to provide easy access to the realm of the dead. Some Native American tribes went as far as burning the deceased house and all of their possessions to escape the wrath of a vengeful ghost.

Archeologists have also discovered burials with decapitated heads, their faces smashed, several bones removed or their arms or legs severed. Massive stones were placed on the body at some sites. They took these additional measures in an attempt to prevent the departed from coming back to the land of the living. Researchers have concluded that these burials were of people whom residents feared in life. How could they return to haunt the living if their bodies are destroyed?

Bottom line, providing the proper burial rites appears to be more of a desire of the living to protect themselves from these unruly spirits than a farewell and sendoff for their dearly departed.

The date when this belief first formed may be pushed back even further by a recent archeological find. In 2013, the fossilized remains of at least 15 individuals were discovered deep within an intricate cave system about 31 miles (50 km) northwest of Johannesburg, South Africa in a room called the *Dinaledi* chamber. The position of the Dinaledi chamber is at the bottom of a narrow chute about 90f (30m) below the surface and about 275f (80m) away from the present cave entrance. These small-bodied hominins, called *Homo naledi*, display a confusing patchwork of features, with some characteristics of the genus *Australopithecus*, while others were more reflective of the genus *Homo*. The fossils discovered date to 236,000 - 335,000 years ago, based on an analysis of the naledi teeth and other measurements performed by the excavating team.

The astonishing thing, other than the discovery of a new breed of hominins, is the suggestion that these early relatives displayed an exclusively human behavior. Researchers have concluded that the bodies found deep within the cave system were intentionally buried. An assemblage of clues has led them to this remarkable supposition. The bones found at the site defy all conventional explanation for how they could have arrived there. The bones do not exhibit signs of tooth marks, which would suggest an animal brought them in. The notion of floodwater washing the bones into the cave was also ruled out. If floodwater were the agent that transported the bones deep within the cave system, the bones would be scattered randomly across the floor. What the research team found was that some anatomical parts were lying virtually intact with the bones resting in the same position they would have appeared in life (Fig. 50).

Figure 50 - Bones of *Homo naledi* in situ. Image courtesy of Marina Elliot.

The discovery of a second cave containing additional remains of *Homo naledi*, the *Lesedi chamber*, adds to this find. Remarkably, all of the bones found in both enclosures were exclusive to *Homo naledi*. Cross-contamination between the two chambers (the movement of bones between one burial location and the other) was considered, but dismissed by researchers. There are no direct routes between the two bone filled areas making it impossible for artifacts from one location to end up in the other. *"There's a potential that we are looking at some kind of rudimentary cultural practice associated with this widely shared emotion of grief,"* said John Hawks, a

Chapter 9: The Invisible World

paleoanthropologist at the University of Wisconsin at Madison who helped lead the Rising Star Expedition. *"It's telling us that this is something that's very deep in our history as humans."*

The team leader, Wits Professor Lee Berger raises another significant point. If, as the evidence suggests, these individuals were deliberately placed inside the cave system, how did they get there? *"I can't see any other way, other than them going into these remote chambers themselves and bringing bodies in."* To navigate the dark underground passages, Berger suspects they could control fire and used it to light their way.

This recent discovery brings up some interesting points. We have already argued that people interred the dead because they possessed a fervent conviction that its spirit would haunt them if he or she did not receive a proper burial. Did these proto-humans have a similar belief system? Were they protecting themselves from these disruptive unseen forces - vengeful ghosts? If so, where did this concept originate? If, as many suggest, we evolved both physically and socially, then we most likely had already experienced manes, lemures, and larvae. What changed? Why would we suddenly become afraid and feel it imperative to protect ourselves from them? Was this practice (and newfound conviction) yet another part of our early education?

There is a second and perhaps more interesting factor that needs mentioning. In culture after culture, we learn that the land of the dead, the place a soul goes after death is located deep within the Earth, the underworld. The route to the realm of the dead is described as being treacherous and paved with hazards. Could a memory of these early burials be a distorted recollection of this underground realm of the dead? If either of these concepts **IS** the case, do they provide evidence of cultural memory, one that is at least 300,000 years old?

Ancestor Worship

Associated with the concept of ghosts, gods, death, and dying is the notion of ancestor worship although the term *ancestor veneration* is probably a better phrase to use when describing this tradition (Fig. 51). People around the globe practice this strange and peculiar custom. Today, when someone dies, we think of him or her as dead and gone. They cease to exist. We may imagine them living for eternity in a heavenly paradise or combating the fires of hell. Our friends or relatives, once dead, are not able to influence or control us. This concept of life after death is not the case when talking about traditional societies.

Figure 51 –Vietnamese ancestor altar. Image courtesy of Thang Nguyen.

Cultures that practice ancestor veneration believe their deceased relatives have a continued existence long after they die. In this tradition, there is the belief that the living can keep a spiritual connection with the dead. They are included as part of the family. An ancestor is a trusted friend and protector. They were thought to provide guidance and advice. Individuals could ask questions or petition them for help. It was held in some cultures that ancestors could intercede on their behalf or act as an intermediary between themselves and the gods. Some also believed their ancestral spirits had the power to influence the course of events and could provide a group or individual with good fortune.

To this end, ancestors were honored. Sacrifices were performed in their name. Food or other provisions were provided for them. These things were done with the underlying

Chapter 9: The Invisible World

understanding: if their deceased relatives were not cared for, like an unruly ghost, it could bring about ill fortune.

One final note regarding ancestor veneration... Many propose that ancestor worship came into being before the advent of modern religion; that our belief in God or the gods developed from this tradition. Yet, in culture after culture, ancestors were never elevated into the role of a god.

Ancestors were always recognized as being human or of having human form at some point in time. They never appear as or are spoken of as supernatural beings. If the process of transforming ancestral spirits into deities had continued, the pantheon of gods would have to be consistently revised, with cultures adding new gods to the roster all of the time. This is not the case.

Additionally, if the gods were at one time the ghost of a deceased relative, then ancestor veneration would have died out with the rise of the godhood. This is also not what we find. What we encounter is the worship of the dead being practiced right alongside their belief in the gods.

Chapter 10:
The Communion

Ceremonies, rituals and religious rites form the basis of every culture on the planet and shape the foundation of all traditional societies. Members of a group would come together with a common intention - devotion to a higher being, communing with spirit and establishing a connection with god. Ceremonies and rituals were held to ensure success and fortune in life, to appease negative spirits or to uncover the cause of an affliction. Common elements of these blessed events included singing, dancing, animal sacrifices, ritual purification, the donning of body paints and mask all culminating in an opportunity to interact with the divine.

In the western world, when we want to commune with God, we go to a church, temple, mosque or synagogue. We are told that it is in this holy place that God dwells. There we may spend time in quiet contemplation and prayer, taking refuge in the thought that it is within *his home* that our prayers will be answered, or at least listened to. We might also passively participate, with other members of our belief community, in a ritualized service performed by a priest, minister, imam or rabbi.

The nature and essence of religious ritual, outside of the Abrahamic traditions, would seem strange, bizarre and downright otherworldly to a modern observer. When

Chapter 10: The Communion

envisioned from a contemporary context they can appear primitive and savage. Early explorers venturing into uncharted lands around the world viewed their ceremonies as repugnant to common decency and morality (Fig. 52). Through their ignorance and feelings of superiority, they failed to explore the foundations of the native's beliefs, culture, myths and most importantly their gods. What they would have realized, upon further examination, was that the fundamental basis and purpose of all sacred rites, when taken down to their base level, are all the same.

Figure 52 - Spanish explorers land in the New World.

Cultures in North America, for example, have rich religious traditions that include their creation myths and other narratives of how their society came into being. They worship an all-powerful, all-knowing creator god. They also believe in an afterlife and the immortality of the human soul. Their belief system is not too far off from the religious traditions held in the modern western world. Early settlers saw Native Americans as uncivilized, uneducated and immoral, so instead of exploring commonalities, they sought to eliminate all that was different from them. The practice of assimilation into European culture occurred in every indigenous society the *white man* encountered.

Communion with the divine can occur individually or as a group-oriented event. The goal is to enter a dream-like state by going into an ecstatic trance. The intentional production of an altered state of consciousness as a means of connecting with God is a practice common to all religious traditions. Priests, mystics or supplicants direct his or her awareness to this spiritual union through the use of fasting, drumming, dancing, prayer, meditation, and even psychoactive drugs. Isolation and retirement from social affairs are believed to contribute to the attainment of this state. In some cultures sleep deprivation, self-inflicted pain, breathing techniques, extreme physical exercise and abstinence from sex is encouraged or required.

These rituals, abet sounding odd, are practiced in the Catholic Church. They are called penance and mortification. Clergymen and women are known for their celibate lifestyle. They might impose severe fasts on themselves, whip or practice self-flagellation, retire for extended periods of imposed silence or prayer or live in extreme poverty following the path of austerity (Fig. 53).

Individuals such as Mother Teresa, Francis of Assisi, Thomas More, Padre Pio of Pietrelcina as well as many other Christian saints provide accounts of their lives lived in self-sacrifice, austerity or following the practice of mortification. Pope John Paul II in his Apostolic Letter, *Salvici Doloris* states: *"It is suffering, more than anything else, which clears the way for the grace which transforms human souls. Suffering, more than anything else makes present in the history of humanity the powers of the Redemption."*

Figure 53 - Illustration of early church practice of penance and mortification.

It was through the practice of offering their pain and suffering *up to God* that the benefits of abundant spiritual growth and strength could be achieved. Through it, their connection to Christ consciousness and redemption from sin could be realized.

> *What is the reason, why some of the Saints were so perfect and contemplative? Because they labored to mortify themselves wholly to all earthly desires; and therefore they could with their whole heart fix*

Chapter 10: The Communion

themselves upon God, and be free for holy retirement. We are too much led by our passions, and too solicitous for transitory things. We also seldom overcome any one vice perfectly, and are not inflamed with a fervent desire to grow better every day; and therefore we remain cold and lukewarm.

– The Imitation of Christ, Thomas à Kempis

Group ceremonies take on a different flavor. Rituals, it was believed, had the power to create a direct link between the earth plane and the celestial realm. It allowed participants the ability to move between the worlds of matter and spirit. It afforded him the opportunity to travel between the upper and lower worlds, to the world above or to the world below. This ability, to transcend the ordinary, was held by certain individuals within the community who were able to attain this most holy connection. Today, we would call these individuals shaman or medicine men. Shaman master the ability to enter into an ecstatic trance state where they open themselves up to receiving the spirit of a deity, angel, demon or the dead. Thus in the face of misfortune, ceremonies and rituals were held to communicate with the spirit world to find out the cause of an affliction or to appease the spirit(s) in question.

Whilst an experiential state is considered by Sufis as the pathway to becoming 'One with God', there are nonetheless multiple layers of outcomes from the trance state, dependent on the practitioner's knowledge and skill. Sufism teaches that an invisible and sensory world containing supernatural and paranormal phenomena exists which may be perceived by the soul... This higher consciousness gives rise to perceptive capacities beyond that observed by the 'ordinary' five senses. The result is personal and experiential knowledge of a world beyond the physical realms, which lifts the veils between the material and invisible worlds...

Sufis believe that the dissolution of the veils between both worlds is an important technique in achieving re-union with The Divine Spirit by perceiving (knowing) the soul as unattached to the physical universe. In their view, mastery of perceiving invisible realms not only assists the soul's re-union with God, but also assists the soul transcend the physical body at death (and any attachments to a material existence). It also assists the practitioner consciously and voluntarily leave their physical body during meditation and while dreaming.

– Sufis and Trance: Self-Knowledge from Experience and Why Altered States of Consciousness Bring Practitioners Closer to God

Music and dance provide a crucial component of these rituals and is a central feature in tribal cultures from America to Australia. Singing is believed to assist individuals to enter into this specialized altered state of consciousness. Ceremonial songs were sung or chanted. Singing takes the mind away from the egoic self. It distracts us from our inner desire to make things happen. It creates a powerful vibration in the body. It *heats up the spirits*. It calls upon the spirit world, invites them to attend the gathering and ultimately join the ritual.

Dancing also prepared the individual for interacting with their gods. It works alongside music to create the required internal circumstances for communication. Dancers transform the sounds they hear and feel into movement. This movement cleanses the body and mind, clear one's internal environment. It allows the individual to disengage their sense of ego-boundaries and helps them submit entirely to the energy being generated by the music.

Combined, the hypnotic nature of the repeated movements and rhythms has the power to send a person into another level of consciousness. It provides a means by which an ecstatic trance can be attained. The music and dance work to awaken and amplify a kind of spiritual electricity in the body. Thus, the stronger the music, the more enthusiasm placed in it, the greater the strength of the dance. As the vibration rises from the communally shared songs, the energy

Chapter 10: The Communion

Figure 54 - Men's dance in the Sandwich Islands, 1816.

available for healing and entrance into an ecstatic state rises (Fig. 54). Through this heightened and enhanced state of consciousness, spirits would speak through the shaman, even if only for a short time. (We will come back to this topic as we move forward.)

The typical flow of a Bushman healing dance moves from gathering around a fire, singing n|om songs and clapping in syncopated rhythms, waiting to be spiritually heated and awakened by n|om, to the ecstatic crescendo of becoming filled with n|om and sharing it with others. Bushman dancers tremble and shake when charged with n|om. A virtuous circularity is set in motion where music inspires the dance as dance inspires the music, while at the same time heightened emotion inspires ecstatic expression and ecstasy amplifies even more emotional intensity. As the Bushman n|on-kxaosi dance around a circle, a greater

> *circulation of n|om is embodies that, in turn, encircles ancestors and gods. In this sacred place, the Bushmen dance with all their ancestors and gods.*
>
> – Way Of The Bushman, Bradford Keeney, Ph.D. and Hillary Keeney, Ph.D.

This ancient tradition of music and dance was perceived as sacrilegious by westerner explorers. In North America, the U.S. Interior Secretary Henry M. Teller called their religious ceremonies *heathenish*, a sentiment that traveled the globe during the Age of Discovery and the European expansion. This practice, regardless of its efficacy, was quickly banned in many communities around the world. It is amazing that between the outlawing of this observance coupled with the practice of genocide that occurred that we have any knowledge of this custom at all.

Finding God Through Chemistry

Communication with spirit was also achieved through the use of intoxicants and psychoactive drugs called entheogens. Entheogens were used ritually to experience the divine and have inspired spiritual experiences throughout history. They were traditionally combined with music and dance to achieve a trance state. They were a part of many religious or shamanic rites. Their use is found in traditional societies in every corner of the planet.

Entheogenic substances are chemical compounds that when ingested change brain function. They act primarily upon the central nervous system, resulting in short-term changes in perception, mood, consciousness, and behavior. They include

Chapter 10: The Communion

intoxicating fermented beverages as well as plants that have narcotic, stimulant and hallucinogenic properties.

The priestess of Apollo in Dieras, for example, became *possessed* by a god and obtained the power of prophecy by drinking the blood of the sacrificial animal. Frank Byron Jevons, in his book *An Introduction to the History of Religion*, describes events among the Fijians after the priest anointed himself with scented oil.

> *In a few minutes he trembles slight distortions are seen in his face and twitching movements in his limbs. These increase to violent muscular action which spreads until the whole frame is strongly convulsed, and the man shivers as with an ague fit. The priest is now possessed by his god, and all his words and actions are considered no longer his own, but those of the deity who has entered into him.*
>
> – An Introduction to the History of Religion,
> Frank Byron Jevons

The use of psychoactive plants may have a longer history than the use of alcohol. According to the article *Psychotropic Substance-seeking: Evolutionary Pathology or Adaptation?*, researchers R. J. Sullivan & E. H. Hagen state: *"As Aborigines had lived in Australia for at least 40,000 years before the arrival of colonists, the antiquity of the exploitation of these native plants may be considerable. "*

At the time of European contact, the Aborigines exploited the indigenous plants *pituri* (Duboisia hopwoodii) and a native *Nicotiana*. Both are high in the chemical compound nicotine. The initial effect of chewing pituri is a stimulant. Pituri, in small quantities, diminishes hunger. It energizes its users thus alleviating physical stress. This characteristic enabled them to undertake long journeys without fatigue and travel with little need for food. It was also employed to stimulate individuals before fighting and to gain visionary powers (Fig. 55).

Evidence suggests the chewing of *betel nut* (Areca catechu) began as early as 13,000 years ago in Timor, and 10,700 years ago in Thailand. Betel nuts, when chewed along with the betel leaves, offer mild stimulant properties and heightened alertness. *Khat* (Catha edulis), which has stimulating properties similar to cocaine, was ingested ritually in Ethiopia and north-east Africa as a means to understand the sacred wisdom of the gods. Likewise, evidence suggests that *coca* (Erythroxylum coca) was being domesticated in the Andes 7000 years ago, and in Ecuador to at least 5000 years ago.

Figure 55 - Chief Sarili Kreli of the Gcaleka; 1890.

Singing, dancing and the drinking *ayahuasca* would send the shaman of South America into a trance-like state. Here they could communicate with nature or the spirit world. Shaman also used it to see what was causing a patient's illness on a spiritual level. The effects of ayahuasca include altered states of consciousness and visual and auditory stimulation. It also offers the user the opportunity to enter into a profoundly introspective state that can lead to elation, illumination and at times profound states of fear.

Today, the plant ayahuasca is used in healing retreats to help cure mental and physical illness through contact with the spirit world. Like ancestral customs, prohibitions are imposed before its use, which can include ritual purification and dietary restrictions such as abstaining from heavily-seasoned foods, excessive fat, salt, and caffeine. Abstinence from sex, before or

Chapter 10: The Communion

after the ceremony, is also required. What other restrictions were obligatory before the consumption of ayahuasca in antiquity are unknown.

The *acacia tree*, like the intoxicating ayahuasca plant, contains the high amounts of the active consciousness altering component *dimethyltryptamine* (DMT). Native to Australia, there are over 1,400 species of Acacia plants. They are distributed in tropical, subtropical and warm temperate parts of the world, including Africa, Asia, the Americas, Australia and the Pacific region.

A species of *Acacia Nilotica*, for example, is portrayed in Egyptian cosmology where it is referred to as the *Tree of Life*. The god Osiris is believed to live inside the acacia tree, a belief similarly held by Amazonian shaman.

Figure 56 - God appears to Moses on the top of Mount Sinai.

Professor Benny Shanon, in his article *Biblical Entheogens: A Speculative Hypothesis*, suggests that Moses' encounter with the burning bush and his subsequent conversation with God occurred because Moses was under the influence of DMT. He put forward that the burning bush was, in reality, an acacia tree (Fig. 56).

Shaman also received insights through the consumption of psilocybin or *magic* mushrooms. Algerian murals that date from 9000 to 7000 BC depict images of psilocybin mushrooms. Small sculptures found in Central and South America that were constructed 2500 to 3000 years ago also suggest their ritual use.

Drumming and dancing were traditionally used in Siberia to achieve a trance state. On occasion, as an alternative method of achieving this state was through the use of the mushroom *A. muscaria* (Amanita muscaria). Interestingly, in eastern Siberia, a shaman would ingest the mushrooms and others would drink his urine. The active constituents of A. muscaria, unlike many other psychoactive substances, pass through the body into the urine unaltered. It is thought by some to be even more potent than the mushrooms themselves.

R. Gordon Wasson, in his work *Soma: Divine Mushroom of Immortality* suggested that the intoxicating drink of the Hindu gods *Soma*, as described in the Indian *Rig Veda*, was a form of A. muscaria. He came to this conclusion based on descriptions provided of the Soma plant in these ancient texts. The final piece of evidence for Wasson was the fact that Soma could be ingested in two forms. One could eat the raw mushroom or drink the urine of someone who had. This quality is unique to A. muscaria.

Peyote is another plant that can cause intense hallucinations. Used by Native Americans, specimens have been found in grave sites dating back to 3000 BC; thou its use may have commenced as early as 10,000 years ago. *Jimson Weed* (Datura stramonium), or *Hell's Bells*, was used in both India and Central America as part of sacred ceremonies. The effects of this potent entheogen have been described as a living dream. The altered state it produces can last for days.

The above are only a few of the consciousness-altering plants and beverages that have been used by cultures worldwide and throughout history. The number of substances that have entheogenic properties is vast. They include beer, fruit wines, rice wine, mead, koumiss, pulque, chicha, morning glories seeds, mescal beans, cohoba, coca, Virola snuffs, tobacco, San Pedro cactus, iboga, kat, cannabis, nightshade plants, opium poppy, and ephedra.

Chapter 10: The Communion

Animal Sacrifice: The Blood Ritual

Blood sacrifices were a common element in sacred ceremonies. Ritual sacrifice goes hand in hand with traditional beliefs and is allied with the earliest form of worship, *animism*. It was an integral part of their culture and was a component of their religious and social obligations. Sacrifices were always tied to a holiday and no holiday would be complete without a sacrifice. They were occasions of joy and emphasized social community. Cultures have practiced this complex phenomenon in all parts of the world.

The most widespread form of ritual sacrifice is the ceremonial killing of an animal although the taking of a man or woman was not unheard of. These live offerings to the gods were commonly performed to appease or maintain favor with the divine, yet the original purpose of this seemingly strange tradition may be even more complicated than that.

Today we view cultures that still practice blood sacrifice as barbaric. We see it as a senseless activity and look down our noses at its apparent savagery. Researchers believe that ritual sacrifice is older than the use of fire and far older than the development of agriculture and the domestication of animals. Large varieties of animals have served as sacrificial offerings over the millennia. They included birds, wild animals, and certain fish. In later times, added to the list were domestic animals such as goats, rams, bulls, oxen, and horses.

The animals associated with some of the oldest blood sacrifice traditions were tied to a clan's totem. Totem animals are conceived of as the symbolic representation of a god or even as an incarnation of the deity himself on Earth. Totem animals were sacred, and the casual killing of one of these revered creatures was taboo and in some cultures was a capital offense.

Animals chosen for this holy rite were slaughter by a variety of specific and ritualized procedures. Piercing the animal with a sword or spear, impaling or dismembering the sacrificial beast was common. Some animals were hung or drowned in a local river or stream. Some cultures indicate that depending on which deity they wished to commune with, the animal and method used to kill it would change. In antiquity, all the gods had animals associated with them. The Greek god Zeus was tied to the eagle, the Sumerian Murdock, the bull and Indra, a Hindu god, the elephant. Thus, if they were hoping to appease a water deity, such as Poseidon, the sacrificial animal would be drowned.

This tradition was so important and so integral to a group's beliefs that countless holy texts commemorate it. Many contend that chapter eight of the book of Genesis offers the first mention of animal sacrifice in the Bible. In it, Noah offers animal sacrifices to God on Mount Ararat after surviving the flood that devastated humanity. *"And Noah built an altar to Jehovah; and took of every clean animal, and of all clean fowl, and offered up burnt-offerings on the altar."* - Genesis 8:20. This belief does not take into account the plant, and animal offerings (sacrifices) of Cain and Abel found in Genesis 4. The Bible, like many ancient traditions, also does not offer a reason why the practice of animal sacrifice began. Did the gods request it?

The Old Testament is filled with a vast number of specific laws and procedures associated with ritual killing. Only unblemished animals of the highest quality were to be used. This requirement, when fulfilled, made the holy gift acceptable and effective. The animals, once selected, were burnt upon an altar of unhewn stones. *"Thou shalt build the altar of the LORD thy God of unhewn stones; and thou shalt offer burnt-offerings thereon unto the LORD thy God."* - Deuteronomy 27:6. The kind and number of animals utilized in the many required sacrifices were extreme and the method employed to perform the various rituals carefully stipulated (See sidebar: *Required Animal Sacrifices In The Old Testament*). The text, in its ongoing narrative, demonstrates the bloodlust of the biblical god.

Chapter 10: The Communion

> ## Required Animal Sacrifices In The Old Testament
>
> The burnt offering must be continued every morning and every evening - Exodus 29:38; Numbers 28:3-8.
>
> At the fulfillment of his vow the Nazirite must present it before God and offer it upon the altar through the priest - Numbers 6:14,16.
>
> On the Sabbath, two lambs - Numbers 28:9.
>
> On the first of the month, two bullocks, one ram and seven lambs - Numbers 28:11.
>
> On the day of first-fruits, the same - Numbers 28:27.
>
> On the 1st day of the 7th month, one bullock, one ram, seven lambs - Numbers 29:8.
>
> On the 15th day, 13 bullocks, two rams, 14 lambs, the number of bullocks diminishing daily until the 7th day, when seven bullocks, two rams, 14 lambs were offered - Numbers 29:12-34.
>
> On the 22nd day of this month one bullock, one ram and seven lambs were offered - Numbers 29:35,36.
>
> – International Standard Bible Encyclopedia, James Orr, M.A., D.D.

The Hindu Vedas mention animal sacrifices throughout its text. In the Sanskrit text, the *Yajurveda*, worshipers would sacrifice a bull to the god Indra. A white goat was offered to the god Vayu and a calf to the god Sarasvati. A speckled ox was presented to Savitr and a castrated ox to Varuna. In some rituals, although not limited to the Hindu tradition, mantras and prayers were offered as part of the ceremony. These rites ranged from the simple killing of an animal to very elaborate affairs.

Regardless of where we look or what culture we explore, it seems apparent that God approved of this method of worship. In the Old Testament, we find the phrase *"an offering made by fire, an aroma pleasing to the LORD"* used over and over in connection with this sacrificial rite. This sentiment is reflected by cultures worldwide. Joseph Samuel Exell, in his book *Biblical Illustrator, Volume 1* notes, *"If sacrifices have not their origin in their inherent reasonableness or in any common affection of the human mind, they must have had their origin in some other authoritative appointment to which all men in common felt constrained to yield."*

Altars of the old world religions were used to receive the blood of the sacrificial animal. They started out as a mere heap of stones. The sacrificial blood was then sprinkled or dashed upon a rough monolithic pillar, or a wooden pole stuck upright in the ground. The pillar was a visible symbol of the deity or was considered the embodiment of the god himself. It was through the monolith that the gods were made manifest. The placing of blood, oil, rendered fat or in some cultures milk on it caused the stone to speak.

Figure 57 - Mayan relief sculpture found in the ancient site of Copan, now Honduras.

As time progressed, and races became more civilized, the altar was transformed from a heap of stones into a more elaborate and artistic structure with a stone table on top. The monolith changed from being the embodiment of a god to merely a physical representation (idol) of the god. Thus, the god who at one time was made manifest in the monolith soon became solely identified with the cold inanimate stone (Fig. 57).

Chapter 10: The Communion

> *As the idol grows more artistic, this practice is discontinues and it is the alter alone on which the blood is sprinkled. Then a house is build for the new god, in which his treasures may be stored. The idol, which from the value of its materials and workmanship is precious is removed into the temple and the alter, now separated from the idol, remains where it was and the slaughter of the victim and the sprinkling of the alter with blood are therefore done outside the temple.*
> – An Introduction to the History of Religion,
> Frank Byron Jevons

As this sacred rite became more ritualized, the focus of this consecrated act shifted from communion and communication with the gods to something that the gods demanded in payment for their continued blessings. Ritual sacrifices, as time progressed, were used to placate the gods in the case of disaster or as a way of removing sin (taboos). Likewise, totem animals lost their sacredness, and the rite became an ambiguous offering to a distant deity that could only be accomplished through an intermediary, a priest. This holy and sacred event moved from being at the very foundation of a community, where the entire group could interact with the divine, into a restricted, controlled and orchestrated affair.

In ancient and traditional cultures, all sacrifices were public affairs. The meat of a sacrificial animal was a vital component of the sacred meal. Sacrificial meals were different from ordinary eating. People ate the fruits of an animal (milk, eggs, honey), without hesitation. The animals themselves, however, were holy and were never killed. Their meat was forbidden and was only eaten on solemn occasions. Each member of the community was required to participate in this sacred meal. It was a communal act, one in which the gods and his worshipers ate together.

It was considered sacrilegious to leave any remains of the sacrificial animal behind. In some cultures, the entire animal was consumed, body, bones, skin, and blood. If something was left over, it was carefully disposed of by burning, burying it or even tossing it into the sea. These measures eliminated the possibility of community members accidentally coming into contact with something sacred. They also feared that any remnants could be used by an enemy if it were to enter into their possession. They could manufacture a magical charm, which could be used to produce illness, ill fortune or worse to those who participated in the feast.

The foundational beliefs held by traditional cultures regarding animal sacrifices seem beyond our realm of understanding. They believe that their involvement in this holy mystery through the ritual death and eating of a sacrificial animal established a holy bond between themselves and their deity. It helped them to enter into communion with their gods. Seen as barbaric and sacrosanct, the essence of this ritual still exists in Western culture through the body and blood of Christ.

The Human Canvas

Body painting is another aspect of many religious rites and ceremonies. The practice of adorning the body with detailed geometric patterns has deep spiritual meanings for groups around the world. Images can range from merely smearing clay or other natural substances onto the body to creating painstakingly precise designs that are applied to the face, limbs, and torso. Body painting helps to identify an individual, who he is and what his role is within the community. Some cultures frown upon the use of body painting while others suggest body art helps to identify humans from non-humans, humankind from the animal world.

Chapter 10: The Communion

Body painting was not done by oneself but was a communal process. The images and symbols that covered the body held implicit meaning. Specific symbols may be used for a particular ceremony, as might the colors that were applied. Stringent guidelines were often followed that dictated the appropriate pattern and even how the paint was to be put on (Fig. 58).

Figure 58 - South African woman applying ritual body paint.

The most common pigment employed to paint the body was red ochre, but yellow ochre, charcoal (black), fire ash, chalk or limestone (white) were also commonly used. These colors are reminiscent of the Mayan creation myth that describes how humanity was created out of corn: red, white, yellow and black. Other materials ranging from roots to berries to tree bark have all been utilized to make dyes. Animal fats, butter or milk, were typically mixed with the pigments to ensure that they would stay on the body, especially since many ceremonies lasted for several days.

The use of ochre has a long history. Evidence suggests that the earliest ochre mine dates back to 350,000 - 400,000 years ago at the Wonderwerk Cave in South Africa. At the site of Terra Amata in France, pieces of ochre were found in association with Acheulian tools. This site dates to some 300,000 years ago. Wear marks on these lumps of ochre indicate that *Homo erectus* had utilized this naturally occurring mineral. (ET Chronicles – The Fight For Immortality)

In Sibudu Cave, a rock shelter in northern Kwazulu-Natal, Africa, an international research team discovered an ochre-based paint that was mixed with milk (animal fat). This find suggests that the practice of body painting, as is still practiced by many cultures today, was in use at least 49,000 years ago. In the Kingdom of Swaziland, South Africa is a site called *Lion Cavern*. Researchers conservatively dated the mining activities that took place at this location to minimally 43,000 years ago. They go on to inform us at over the course of its long history at least 100,000 tons of ochre have been removed from this location.

Skeptics assert that iron oxide (ochre) had a variety of alternative purposes outside of ritual use. They suggest that hunter-gatherer societies utilized ochre medicinally for its antiseptic qualities, as a food preservative, to tan hides, as a sunscreen and even as an insect repellent. The applications identified by cynics do hold merit. Ochre, in some contemporary cultures, is still used for these purposes, but the archeological record also shows us another use.

Ochre went hand in hand with funerary rites. In Australia, at Lake Mungo, in Western New South Wales, excavated burial sites have yielded ochre-covered bones. Carbons dating of the bones indicate these individuals lived approximately 62,000 years ago. Dr. Dennis O'Neil, Professor Emeritus of Anthropology and Behavioral Sciences at Palomar College in San Marcos, California informs us:

> *By 90,000 years ago, several Neanderthal cave sites provide the first reasonably good evidence of intentional burial of their dead. They presumably buried relatives and friends in shallow graves dug into the soft midden soil of their living areas at the mouths of caves and rock shelters. Usually the bodies were flexed in a fetal position. Frequently, the bones were stained with hematite, a rust-red iron ore [ochre]. It is likely that the bodies were either sprinkled with hematite powder or the powdered pigment was mixed*

Chapter 10: The Communion

with a liquid medium, such as vegetable seed oil, and painted on the bodies.
– Evolution Of Modern Humans: *A Survey of the Biological and Cultural Evolution of Archaic and Modern Homo sapiens,* Dennis O'Neil

The Face of God

Facial masks were also an integral part of many rituals. Masks are a familiar part of our contemporary culture and are a dramatic element worn during theatrical productions, festivals, celebrations, parties and even on Halloween. They are a fun and festive way of disguising our true identity, but in traditional cultures, masks were objects of reverence. They played an essential role in their social and religious life and were reserved for a select few who had permission to wear them.

Masks have been utilized by traditional cultures worldwide from time immemorial and have been made of a variety of materials including leather, wood, bark, skin, cloth, bone, vegetable materials, stone, and gold. They depict human faces, animals, spirits, venerated ancestor, specific gods or the heads of mythological creatures. The oldest masks, purported to have been discovered in the Judean desert, are 9000 years old and are made of stone (Fig. 59). There are 11 of these Neolithic stone masks. Many believe that the practice of mask-making is much older than

Figure 59 - 9000 year old Neolithic stone mask.

these extremely early finds. It can be concluded, based upon the customary materials used to make masks that remnants of this primeval practice are long gone, having deteriorated years ago.

Shaman, in sacred ceremonies, would often wear a mask. They had the power to help the shrouded individual shed his physical form. It transformed him into someone or something else, be it an ancestor, an animal or even a god. They supported the wearer as they left this world behind and journeyed into the land of spirits. They paved the way for the masked individual to be recognized in the land beyond. Peter and Roberta Markham in their book *Masks of the Spirit*, take this concept one step further. They suggest that masks when incorporated into a location, for example on a cave wall, on the side of a building or hung on the wall, help the shaman gain access into the hidden realms where his teachers reside.

Some masks were manufactured and covered the head and face. Others were painted on the body. It was not uncommon for someone to be disguised from head to toe with what might be regarded as a costume today. Masks supported the transformational ability of the wearer. They were an essential part of many time-honored ceremonies and were fabricated for specific ritual events. These events included marriage, initiation, healing, planting, harvesting, hunting and preparation for war.

Masks have also been long associated with the transition from life to death and were a critical part of many funerary rites. The ancient Egyptians took the creation and use of ritual death masks to an all-time high. How many of us can readily recall images of the majestic gold mask worn by King Tutankhamun (King Tut)? His facepiece, made of solid

Figure 60 - Death mask of King Tutankhamun.

gold constitutes one of the most well-known death masks in the world (Fig. 60).

Masked characters, as part of a funerary service, help transport the spirit of the dead onto their next life. Death masks helped the deceased pass more readily into the afterworld and prevented them from becoming trapped in this world only to wander the Earth for eternity. Unlike traditional ritual masks, which magically transformed an individual into the role of a god, the *god impersonator*, death masks transformed the deceased into a god himself. He could then experience eternal life, something his physical body was unable to do. The mask also allowed the gods to recognize him allowing him to take his rightful place among the other celestial deities. (ET Chronicles - The Fight For Immortality)

The Sacred Caribberie

We have explored the varied components that make up holy ceremonies, ones that transcend world cultures. In modern times we have lost the real intention, dynamic, feeling, and purpose of them. Traditional societies used them to achieve an ecstatic state and commune with spirit. The ecstatic experience underlies every religion on the planet. They say tradition dies hard and to have a relationship with God is no exception. It appears, however, that as cultures advanced, instead of creating a stronger union with the divine, we have become distant. We find ourselves going through a set of hollow rituals that only vaguely represent their original objective. They have become powerless and devoid of meaning and purpose.

Sacred rituals were not arbitrary endeavors. They were not casually observed like a child's christening or celebrated in the way we commemorate Christmas or the 4th of July. Everything

Stepping Out of Eden

about them was well planned and executed. For the citizens of a traditional society, their lives and the welfare of the community were at stake.

Early ethnographers, when studying these cultural groups, only reported on the external experience, the task at hand, the components of a ceremony or ritual. They described the barbaric animal sacrifices, the obscene dancing, the incessant sounds of the pounding drums and the unintelligible singing (Fig. 61). What they failed to describe was the most crucial part of the entire celebration - the ecstatic experience itself. They did not recognize or failed to comment on the fact that the cleansing, fasting, singing, and dancing was all done to prepare individuals for their connection with spirit. Instead, this most sacred, most holy and most important part of the observance was deemed irrelevant and was ultimately ignored.

Figure 61 - Fijians partaking in sacred rites.

By taking all of these individual components, the singing, the dancing, the communal painting and decorating process and deciphering how they tie together, we might be able to gain some insights into this ancient practice.

It could take a week or more, in many cultures, to prepare for the commencement of sacred rites. Ritual cleansing, fasting, and other preparatory practices would begin long before the festivities would commence. Masks were fashioned; body paints were made and applied. The location where the ceremony was to take place was cleansed and sanctified. Special foods and offerings to the gods or ancestral spirits were prepared. All was done to set the stage for the climax of the festival - the *Sacred Caribberie*.

Chapter 10: The Communion

    The whole community would gather together after all of the preparations were complete. The aroma of aromatic plants filled the air, setting the stage for the festivities to come. Finally, a sacrificial animal was slaughtered; its spilled blood would open the door to the spirit world. The drummers would begin beating out ancient rhythms while others sang or chanted. A symbolic dance would commence with the dancers moving in harmony to the rhythmic beat. Intoxicating substances (if applicable) were consumed. As the drumbeat intensified, so would the movement of the dancers. In the seemingly increasing frenzy of music and dance, select participants would lose themselves to its hypnotic rhythm. Those who had achieved this altered state of consciousness could now surrender their egos and step outside of time and space. They could begin their journey climbing the rope of perception and enter the world of spirit.

    The shaman would first encounter geometric patterns and designs as they made their way up the rope. Researchers Tom Froese, Alexander Woodward, and Takashi Ikegami, who studied 40,000 years of cave paintings, in their article, *Turing Instabilities In Biology, Culture, And Consciousness? On The Enactive Origins Of Symbolic Material Culture*, suggest that the commonalities in the geometric patterns and images depicted on cave walls did not just pop up by coincidence but show a consistency of visual experience tied to altered states of consciousness.

    Test individuals who had taken hallucinogenic drugs would encounter spiral-like, labyrinth and fractal designs including spots, traveling waves, grids, and spirals that parallel motifs recorded on cave walls. They go on to propose that these images were a direct result or somehow tied to sacred rites and the ecstatic experience. Test patients of Dr. Rick Strassman, in his government-sanctioned clinical trials into the effect of the psychoactive compound DMT, experienced similar geometric designs. The documentary *DMT: The Spirit Molecule* records their experiences.

Figure 62 - Representation of Anubis located at Deirel-Bahari. Image courtesy of Hedwig Storch.

Finally, once high enough up the rope, they would be propelled into what the San people of Africa call the *First World*. The aborigines of Australia call this ecstatic state the *Dreamtime*. Their ancestral spirits, teacher, and gods live in this reality. According to Bradford Keeney & Hillary Keeney, the author of the book *Way Of The Bushman*, the first world existed before the naming of things. It is a realm of pure energy or pure being. It existed before the solid form we find in our 3-dimensional world. *Reality* in this dimension is not firm or locked down, but ever changing, moving and flowing. Individuals who experience this realm find it hard to put words to their experiences, not because they cannot, but because we do not have words to describe it in our current vocabulary.

In the fluidity of this space, it has been reported, for example, that elements of men can interchange with aspects of animals and they with us. Uncanny and hard to believe as this may sound, Graham Hancock, in his book *Supernatural: Meetings With the Ancient Teachers of Mankind* details his own and other's experiences with psychoactive drugs. They too, like the San people, testify to this transformative phenomenon.

Both authors contend that the ever-changing shape-shifting quality of individuals encountered in the first world (therianthropes) is reflected in our early art. The Keeney's point to the art of Egypt where the jackal-headed god Anubis (Fig. 62) and the ibis-headed god Thoth are visual examples of this metamorphic transformational state. The gods can change from human in appearance, to hybrid-like, to appearing in full animal form. Hancock suggests that ancient cave art also displays this transfigured state, where images such as *The Sorcerer* found in the *Cave of the Trois-Frères*, in France, is seen as an example (Fig. 63).

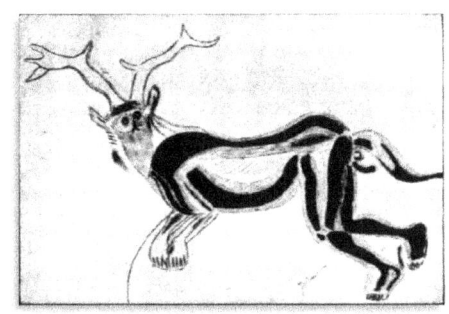

Figure 63 - The Sorcerer, located in the Cave of the Trois-Frères.

Select individuals would be taken over by spirit once an ecstatic trance was achieved. We refer to this kind of interaction with spirit as a *possession*. When we think of possession, we may recall images of Regan in the movie *The Exorcist* as she spoke in a demonic voice, levitated off her bed and had her head spin around 360 degrees. What we fail to recognize is that the overcoming of the body with spiritual energy has and still does appear in many modern-day forms of evangelical Christianity, primarily when a person speaks in tongues. They are filled with the *Holy Ghost* who takes possession of the believer. The concept of being overcome by a spirit during a sacred rite is no different.

When a spirit enters an individual, he or she loses all consciousness. The spirit displaces the host's personality and takes over their physical body. The traits and behaviors of the invited spirit will often manifest in the mannerisms of the host. Some spirits are gentle. Others are stronger, more energetic and even aggressive. Older spirits may leave the individual seeming frail, weak or infirm. If the entering spirit was disabled in life, this disability might also be displayed. Even the individual's facial expressions may change and more closely resemble the spirit of a god, goddess or ancestor. Interestingly, specific songs, rhythms, masks and even body paints had the power to summon a particular spirit to the ceremony who would hopefully make its presence known to the group.

Members of the community could make requests of the spirits once an individual was overcome. They could ask for guidance or healing. These divine beings would educate the community by imparting insights, advice, warnings and even prophecies. The festivities would begin after their communion with the gods concluded. Eating and drinking would commence, and the village would share in the sacrificial meal. At the conclusion of the ritual celebration, body paint was smeared or obliterated. Any designs on the ground destroyed. It would be only too soon before the rigors of everyday life would be upon them again. The guidance, blessings, and insights offered, however, would be used to direct the community in the days, weeks and months that followed.

The Ecstatic Experience: A Modern View

The ecstatic experience sounds eerie, yet this same skill can be explained using a more fashionable vernacular. Contemporary western thought suggests that only specific individuals such as mystics, psychics, channels, and mediums can access this unseen realm. What traditional cultures worldwide recognize is that you do not have to possess special powers to interact with it. This vibratory information is there for the taking but is filtered and hidden from our view by our cognitive reality, our egos and through the constructs society places upon us. People who actively look to access this sphere of existence today typically engage in a spiritual practice such as meditation, yoga, introspection, praying, chanting and rituals.

Chapter 10: The Communion

Spiritual practices, like meditation, work by helping us shake loose the negative thoughts and limiting beliefs we cling to. We have all had the experience of letting go of trapped energy. Perhaps, after a workout at the gym, you found yourself leaving the facility feeling physically refreshed but also experiencing a deep sense of peace within yourself. Maybe dancing, singing, creating a piece of art, walking, jogging or reading a book offers you this quality. For some, even raking leaves, washing dishes or cleaning a bathtub can provide the freeing properties a meditative practice offers.

Great importance was placed upon the performance of ceremonies in traditional societies. Ritual IS a meditative practice. Just about every aspect of a ritual when done correctly or *with feeling* supports internal cleansing. Similar to the intense concentration used by Tibetan monks as they construct an intricate sand-painted mandala (Fig. 64), the grinding and applying of body paints can be meditative.

Figure 64 - Tibetan Buddhist monks create mandala sand painting.

The same holds true with the creation of ceremonial masks, ritual cleansing and the preparation of the land and food offerings. These observances benefited the participants and supported the community at large. They worked to cleanse the energetic body of trapped thoughts and emotions and bring about a sense of peace while preparing their psyches for working with these unseen forces.

Ritual allowed these populations to stay closer to this magical state much like an intense, ongoing meditative practice does for many today. In this cleansed, energized state, according to Australian researchers Steven and Evan Strong, Australian Elders demonstrate the capability of communicating with animals, trees and the whole of nature, a skill often recounted in world myth. And this is just the tip of the iceberg when talking about the abilities available to individuals when in this highly charged condition. One can only assume that at one time all of humanity lived in a vastly different state of consciousness.

Recent scientific studies have brought forth information that supports the power of rituals and the associated ecstatic experience. To start, our brain operates within five different frequency ranges. Each range affects our consciousness.

Delta waves (0.5 Hz to 3 Hz) oscillate at the lowest frequency. They are associated with sleep and sleeping and by the appearance of a seemingly unconscious state, which includes the loss of physical awareness.

Theta waves (4 Hz to 7 Hz) appear during sleep but are also dominant in deep meditation. It acts as our gateway to learning and memory. In theta, our senses withdraw from the external world. They are linked to day-dreaming, memory recall, and guided visualization. When we are in theta, we can access information beyond our normal waking consciousness.

Alpha waves (8 Hz to 13 Hz) are the resting state of the brain. Alpha waves aid overall mental coordination, calmness, alertness, mind/body integration and learning. When in them, our internal dialog gets turned off, and we can be in the present moment in a place of peace and relaxation. Our bodies naturally move into alpha waves when we are relaxed or during certain forms of meditation.

Beta waves (12 Hz to 28 Hz) are the waves associated with daily activity and our waking consciousness. We are alert and engaged in a focused mental activity, although anxiety or excitement can appear when we are in this brain state. Some suggest beta waves support automated endeavors where we move through life without any creativity or inventiveness.

Chapter 10: The Communion

Gamma waves (40 Hz to 100 Hz) are most often recorded during times of intense creative work and when we encounter sudden bursts of inspiration. Researchers speculate that gamma rhythms modulate perception and consciousness. They are the fastest of brain waves and allow us to simultaneous process information from different areas of the brain.

Recent studies have uncovered that our planet exhibits a series of low-frequency electromagnetic fluctuations (ELF) with the primary frequency resonating at 7.83Hz. This rhythmic wave has been likened to the heartbeat of the Earth. It plays a significant role in our physiological functions and is crucial to our body's ability to relax physically and mentally. We are evolutionarily attuned to this vibration and have come to rely on it to maintain our internal biorhythms and maintain health.

Studies have shown that if a new frequency is introduced into our environment *brain-wave entrainment* can occur. Brainwave entrainment, or brainwave synchronization, refers to the capacity of the brain to naturally match the rhythm of external stimuli. Our bodies will automatically *tune into* (entrain) this new signal. When the mantra OM is chanted, many readily achieve a relaxed alpha state. OM, the cosmic hum, resonates at the frequency of 7.83 Hz.

Research also indicates that when a group meditates, their brains begin to entrain with one another and their surroundings, providing them with an elevated and more profound experience. The drums, chants, singing, and dancing performed by participants during a ritual help connect them in a shared experience by synchronizing their brainwave activity with one another. According to James L. Kent, author of *Psychedelic Information Theory: Shamanism in the Age of Reason*, "*If the shaman and the ritual participants all sing the same tones together, their oscillators all merge into a constructive interference pattern and drive each other into a higher amplitude of shared energy. This is the physics of neural entrainment and linking group mind.*"

Sacred songs set a vibratory tone. Their rhythms, along with their associated dance, entrain the group into a unique resonant frequency. They guide them into a relaxed alpha state, while the distinct vibratory tone acts like a calling card inviting a particular god, ancestor or spirit to the celebration.

John Kounios and Mark Beeman, in their study of the *Aha! Moment* (those fleeting moments of profound insight), detected high bursts of gamma brainwave activity just before a new idea or insight entered into the consciousness of their volunteers. Alpha brainwave activity typically preceded the gamma bursts. Neuroscientist Richard Davidson's 2004 study on the energy emitted by Tibetan meditating monks reported that some of the monks had more powerful and higher amplitude gamma wave activity than any other group on the planet. In their 2005 study on the effects of the entheogen dimethyltryptamine (DMT), David E. Stuckey, Robert Lawson & Luis Eduardo Luna describe *"increases in global EEG coherence in the 36–44 Hz and 50–64 Hz (Gamma Hz) frequency bands"* of volunteers who had ingested DMT. They found that its use makes test subject more susceptible to entrainment at higher frequency levels and for sustained periods of time.

This information suggests that rituals were used to unite the group mind in a relaxing alpha brainwave state. The increased amplitude created by the group aided the shaman as he climbed the rope to the first world (gamma state) where he would interact with spirit. It also implies that the consumption of entheogens may have helped the shaman access and maintain gamma brainwave activity for extended periods.

Rituals were done intentionally and with a sense of purpose. The community would enter into these sessions with a desire in their hearts, a request in hand or a specific outcome in mind. They were used to say farewell to a loved one, as part of the hunt or warfare, to heal disease, to bring peace and contentment to their group and to celebrate life events.

Myth suggests, as we have explored earlier, that these holy rites and sacred ceremonies were taught to humanity by the gods. Were we trained in a methodology would allow us to

Chapter 10: The Communion

communicate with the spirit world and to the gods themselves? Today, most do not recognize the value of interacting with this other world, yet for thousands of years, hundreds of cultures worldwide have utilized holy rites and sacred plants for this purpose.

Chapter 11:
Man or Myth – The Gods Revisited

Who or what are the gods? Are they as we suggested in Chapter 3, *Who Are The Gods*, living breathing individuals, are they etheric being who can be contacted via the ritual experience or are they the creation of man as scholars suggest? Let us take each on their own merit.

Myth gives the impression that the gods had physical bodies. Around the world, groups readily describe what the gods looked like and acted like. Imagery, based on oral traditions, offers a consistent but distinct set of physical characteristics for the gods. This consistency of representation suggests that independent cultures are all talking about a specific finite assemblage of individuals. (ET Chronicles – A God By Any Other Name)

Figure 65 – Reproduction of Indra's vijra.
Image courtesy of asianart.com.

Although not a god, we can use the weapon wielded by the Sky God Indra as an example. His weapon of choice was

Chapter 11: Man or Myth – The Gods Revisited

the vijra (Fig. 65). Images of his vijra have remained intact in Indian cosmology through the millennia. Representations of a remarkably similar lightning emitting tool, wielded by a Sky God, are also found in cultures, including the Greeks, Sumerians, and Aztecs. Depictions of this device of mass destruction remain virtually intact regardless of which civilization you explore. How could oral descriptions and visual images of a vijra be produced and then transmitted down through the generations if no one ever witnessed this weapon? (ET Chronicles – The Gods & Their Toys)

One thing that we here in the west need to realize is that our belief in a prevailing all powerful and all knowing God clouds our understanding of the olden gods in general. When we look at the gods of other cultures, we envision them through Judeo/Christian lenses and apply our bias to who or what they are. Even the names used to describe what we call the gods are tainted. What we, in the west, call God, the Australian First People refer to as *Sky Heroes*. They are the *Sky People* to many Native American cultures and the Anunnaki (those who from heaven to Earth came) to the Sumerians. These names offer up a far different connotation to the nature of God.

Regardless of if you are talking about an Abramic God, a traditional god, the Sky People, Sky Heroes or Anunnaki, perhaps our understanding of them formed similarly to what is known as the *Cargo Cult* who lived on an island in the South Pacific.

Set between Fiji and New Guinea, is the Oceanian island nation called Vanuatu (formerly New Hebrides). It consists of a group of more than 80 islands in the South Pacific Ocean. The people of New Hebrides were an aboriginal group whose cosmology was based on traditional beliefs. It wasn't until the 1600's that they had their first encounter with Europeans. The natives, as the number of French and English colonists on the Island grew, had minimal contact with these outsiders.

Life in this remote Pacific Island chain changed dramatically with the outbreak of World War II. New Hebrides found itself in a unique position. It was midway between

Australia and the United States and was near the ongoing conflicts that were occurring in the Pacific. It, because of its strategic location, was taken over by hundreds of thousands of American soldiers. They quickly set up forward military bases where they built an airfield and naval portages.

The activities of the newly arrived *Americans* on their isolated island were strange and wondrous to the natives. In an odd twist of fate, what drastically changed the life of the indigenous populations were the vast amounts of supplies that planes airdropped onto the US bases. They observed aircraft descend from the sky and deliver crate after crate each filled with a diversity of sensational treasures, the likes of which the residents had never seen. They were enthralled with the *gifts of the gods*; radios, trucks, boats, watches, iceboxes, medicine, Coca-Cola, canned meat, and candy. They believed that these riches came from the gods who live in the sky. They also learned that the astonishing goods that miraculously came from above were called c*argo*.

The Americans left New Hebrides at the conclusion of WWII. They abandoned the military bases, and the steady flow of airdropped supplies ceased. The men and woman of New Hebrides did not understand why, but they were determined to call upon the sky gods to intervene on their behalf and resume bringing them their phenomenal gifts.

Figure 66 - Bamboo plane constructed by the indigenous culture of New Hebrides

The islanders set to work. They knew the secret of summoning these mysterious ships. They had seen the Americans do it day after day. They created landing strips, constructed control towers, wooden radio headsets and

Chapter 11: Man or Myth – The Gods Revisited

bamboo planes (Fig. 66). Men from the village sat in the towers wearing their mock earphones. Others stood on the runways and waved their version of landing signals. They did all of this to attract the god's attention with the hope that they would drop more of their heavenly wonders on their island. But for some reason, it did not work. No airplanes landed, and cargo never fell from the sky again.

If the indigenous people of New Hebrides mistook cargo ships for the craft of their gods, then if we go further back into our history, what were people observing that was documented in our most ancient legends?

In turn, authors like Graham Hancock have come forward and suggested that the gods did not take on physical form. He and others believe that these non-corporeal beings, these spirits are just that – spirits who live outside of our 3rd dimensional realm. And it is true. Individuals who have experienced an ecstatic state often report of interacting with non-corporeal beings including ancestors, spirits and the gods. They would be encountered during sacred rituals when a shaman climbed the rope of his inner landscape and entered into the first world.

One counterpoint to the gods existing on etheric realms is the concept that the gods ate and drank, had celestial chariots, magical weapons, fought wars and battles, got married and could ultimately die. Stories of interactions with the gods when in an altered state do not include these notions. Perhaps our understanding of life on other dimensional plains is incomplete. It is also possible that the spirits they encounter were not gods at all but were mislabeled by ignorant westerners. How could a ghostly non-corporeal being interact with us on the physical plane anyway? Other than by educating us or providing us with insights and information, would they be able to enact changes in us such as modifying our genetic inheritance?

There are some who suggest that the gods can move through planes of reality, where they can be seen, heard and interact here on the physical plane, but in the same breath can disappear and return to their multidimensional home. This concept would indeed resolve the argument of whether the gods are physical or spiritual beings.

Then there is the final, scientific view that the gods are a creation of humanity. If the gods of traditional cultures were created and used to explain concepts such as natural phenomena and psychological archetypes it does not answer one fundamental question. If the gods are imaginary characters, then why would members of society feel submissive, fear retribution and at the same time revere a fictitious make-believe being? Why experience a sense of obedience to an invisible, unseen imaginary force?

When we look to resolve the problem of whom, or what, the gods are, its resolution is often taken as an all or nothing proposition. God has to be physical, spiritual or fictitious. Based upon the materials in hand, who says that there was only one group of gods? Perhaps, one group interacted with humanity on the physical plane and a separate assemblage on the etheric. Could the gods who created us, the ones who manipulated our DNA and are memorialized in our early myths have taken on a physical form? Likewise, could the gods who are honored, worshiped, venerated and communicated with, as part of a cultures deep ritual tradition, exist on higher dimensional planes, one that can only be accessed through sacred ceremonies?

What our ancestors saw or witnessed is a mystery, but if you take the reaction of the people of New Hebrides as any indicator, it does seem that what we experienced, at least at one point in our history, was real and tangible. Similarly, our ability to communicate with the gods, our ancestors or a vengeful spirit, via the ecstatic experience, has been practiced by individuals in world cultures for millennia.

Chapter 12:
Body Modification

Societies around the world portray distinct characteristics, which define their culture. From the clothes worn, the language spoken and the traditions that are passed from generation to generation, each of these can provide insights into a cultural group. There are, however, a consistent series of customs that are practiced on each continent of the globe. One of these practices is body modification.

Body modification, or body alteration, is the deliberate manipulation of one's physical appearance for non-medical reasons. There are but a few parts of the human body that have not been subjected to some kind of manipulation. Forms of body modification include tattooing, circumcision, body piercing and cranial deformation. Each of these has one thing in common - the changes made to one's appearance are permanent.

The tradition of body modification originated in our remote past. The reason why an individual would permanently alter their physical form vary. Writer and filmmaker, Vince Hemingson, who has studied body modification practices worldwide has observed, "*In almost all hunting and gathering cultures, shedding of blood summons the gods—and good and evil spirits.*" Body modifications were used to mark rites of passage, to celebrate life achievements, to identify an individual's community status or group affiliation, to adorn and beautify the body, to display wealth or to connect with their gods.

It is difficult to explain real beauty. A defect in one country is a desideratum in another. Scars upon the face are, in Europe, a blemish; but here [in central Africa] and in the Arab countries no beauty can be perfect until the cheeks or temples have been gashed.
– In The Heart Of Africa, Samuel Baker

Tattooing

The deliberate marking of the skin was an essential and integrated part of many if not all ancient cultures. These permanent designs have served as amulets, status symbols, declarations of love, signs of religious beliefs, adornments and even forms of punishment.

Linguists believe that the word tattoo was borrowed from the Tahitian word *tatau*, which translates to - *to mark something*. It also appears in the Samoan lexicon where it means *open wound* and in the Polynesian language (hahau) where it denotes *to strike* or *pierce*. Regardless of the word used, a tattoo implies the creation of an indelible mark or figure on the body. They are created by piercing, cutting or inscribing the skin with pointed bones, thorns, needles and inserting colored materials beneath its surface, thus permanently discoloring the skin. From plain, to elaborate, how far back this practice goes is unknown, but the anecdotal and direct evidence associated with tattooing tells us that this tradition is ancient.

Very few stories regarding the origin of tattooing have survived. One Maori myth tells the story of a young warrior

Chapter 12: Body Modification

named Mataora. Mataora fell in love with Niwareka, the princess of a race of Turehu, who lived in the Maori underworld. Mataora and Niwareka were married and lived happily together for a while. One day Mataora, in a fit of rage, struck his wife who ran away and returned home to the underworld. The young couple, resolving their differences, decided to return to the world above. Before they left, Niwareka's father, the King of the Underworld, taught Mataora the art of *ta moko* (tattooing). Mataora brought this skill back to his people.

On the island of Tahiti, legend tells us that the first tattoos were emblazoned on the sons of the god Ta'aroa, the Polynesian supreme creator god. Ta'aroa's sons, Matamata and Tū Ra'i Pō, taught this craft to humankind who used it extensively.

Figure 67 - Lion man of the Hohlenstein Stadel.

Outside of myth and legend, the earliest anecdotal evidence to support tattooing appears in the art of the Paleolithic era in Europe. Found on the left shoulder of the 40,000-year-old *Löwenmensch figurine* or *Lion man of the Hohlenstein Stadel* (Fig. 67) are a series of parallel lines. These lines, according to some researchers of this ancient practice, suggest that tattooing was part of human culture as early as the creative explosion. Addition evidence, from the same period, may be found on the small ivory statue the Venus of Hohle Fels (Fig. 68). This figurine, dated to between

Figure 68 - Venus of Hohle Fels.

35,000 to 40,000 years ago, shows a series of incised lines on her abdomen, chest and both of her arms, which are thought to indicate tattoos.

Suggestive at best, proponents of a tattooing culture during the Paleolithic are met with skepticism. Cynics argue that it is impossible to determine if the inscribed lines seen on these ancient figures are in fact permanent decorations. The marks that appear, they reason, instead of being tattooed emblems, could, in reality, be an indication of body paint or another kind of body art.

The site of *Grotte de Fees* (Fairy Grotto), in Chatelperron, France, may hold some additional evidence of an early tattooing tradition. In 1867, pieces of sharpened flint and bowls containing red and black pigments were discovered. Pots with traces of red ochre and sharp needle-shaped bones have also been found in other sites in France as well as in Scandinavia and Portugal. These discoveries date to about 12,000 years ago. Archaeologists Saint-Just Péquart and Marthe Péquart have suggested that these primitive tools provide conclusive evidence of ancient tattooing. Detractors of the claims made by Saint-Just and Marthe Péquart are quick to point out that these there may be a multitude of uses for these same implements. Agnieszka Marczak in her article *Tattoo World* states:

> *Although these material remains are intriguing, and the archaeologists themselves identified these implements as tattoo tools, we have no tattooed human skin preserved from this time period; therefore, it cannot conclusively be said that these instruments were not used for some other purpose.*
>
> – Tattoo World, Agnieszka Marczak

Tattoo anthropologist, Lars Krutak, argues that the only way to conclusively date the art of tattooing is through direct evidence, namely a tattoo preserved on human skin. The unfortunate nature of permanent body markings is that, unlike a stone tool, the skin begins to degrade shortly after death.

Chapter 12: Body Modification

While many ancient burial sites contain skeletal remains, bodies from prehistoric tombs that still retain their epidermis are rare.

The earliest, although not first, intact tattooed individual was discovered in 1991. Hikers trekking through the Ötztal Alps came across the mummified body of a man frozen in the ice of an ancient alpine glacier. Tests indicated that this man, dubbed the *Iceman* or *Ötzi*, lived about five thousand years ago. One of the remarkable things about Ötzi's is that his body is covered with 61 tattoos. These markings are located on his left wrist, his lower legs, his back, and torso.

The tattoos, surprisingly, are not decorative as one might expect. They are grouped in a series of lines and crosses. They are colored dark blue and are believed to have been made by using soot from a fireplace. The mummified remains of Ötzi are not the only ones that come to us from the remote past. Hundreds of ancient mummies with tattooed bodies have been found in locations such as Egypt, Africa, Europe, China, Siberia, the Philippines, Alaska, Greenland, Mexico, and South America. These worldwide finds indicate how widely practiced and globally encompassing this tradition was. It also implies that the practice of permanently marking the body was well understood and integrated into their communities long before these individuals lived and died.

Tattoos have served a variety of purposes over the years. Unfortunately for us, many of the rights and traditions associated with the art of tattooing, as well as the inherent meaning of the inscribed symbols themselves, have been lost or wiped out by invading modern western civilizations. Thankfully, in a few cultures where there were strong tattooing traditions, early anthropologists had an opportunity to observe this ritual and derive insights into this painful and bloody procedure.

> But those who paint themselves permanently do so with extreme pain, using, for this purpose, needles, sharp awls, or piercing thorns, with which they perforate, or have others perforate, the skin. Thus they

form on the face, the neck, the breast, or some other part of the body, some animal or monster, for instance, an Eagle, a Serpent, a Dragon, or any other figure which they prefer...

– Tattooing among the Petun and Neutrals Indians of Mexico, The Jesuit Relations of 1652

Tattoos were not randomly given. The process of having one's body marked necessitated the drawing of blood. Blood, as we have already discussed, was inherently sacred. Interacting with this divine substance brought along with it a large number of cultural taboos. Dancing, chanting and other ceremonial rites traditionally preceded this sacrosanct practice. The hallowed nature of tattoos required those who were to undergo this procedure fasted, abstained from sexual relations and performed ritual cleansing. It was a serious and celebratory life event, one that was never taken lightly.

Figure 69 - Tattooed Maori chief.

The signs and symbols our ancestors used to adorn their bodies were filled with meaning (Fig. 69). The patterns and their relative placement had significance. Symbols or depictions of animals helped connect the individual with the spirit of their totem animal. The same held true in some cultures with images of their gods. The profound, significance of these symbols, which were once fixed in the minds of our ancestors, is now clouded by speculation, their inherent meanings debated.

There are several reasons why our ancestors got tattooed. Intriguingly, they all fall into a small yet consistent handful of themes. The most common explanation offered for getting a

Chapter 12: Body Modification

tattoo was as an initiatory rite. Pubescent teens, traditionally males, were tattooed as a rite of passage from boyhood to maturity. Young adults, who were not tattooed, were considered *boys* even after puberty. This stigma followed them throughout life. They were seen as having a lower social status. The young man could not get married. He could not participate in the hunt. In some groups, he could not speak in the presence of grown men. He would be branded a coward, and an incomplete tattoo would be a permanent marking of his cowardice. He would become an outcast of the tribe, which would bring shame upon his family.

A tattoo may identify one's genealogy or position in society, an individual's worth or their achievements such as the battles they won or the enemies they killed. Permanent external signs, like tattoos, made it easier to distinguish friend from foe and married versus single. They were believed to make a person more attractive to the opposite sex or appear fierce in battle. In cultures that have strong marriage taboos associated with clan alliance, a tattoo would quickly let an individual know if a potential mate was from an appropriate clan or not.

The act of tattooing spilled blood, so many cultures saw it as a way of contacting or connecting with spirits. They were used as amulets and magical adornments. Some cultures believed their markings could help them pass undisturbed into the afterlife and help them avoid becoming a ghost and wander the earth for eternity. Tattoos are said to aid married couples in finding each other in the spirit world. They also allowed the departed to be recognized by their cultural ancestors in the hereafter. In an ancient Iban proverb, we learn *"a man without tattoos is invisible to the Gods."*

Tattoos were also used in some cultures to brand their slaves and identify criminals. A handful of biblical historians suggest that the mark Cain received on his forehead after killing his brother Able was a tattoo. They go on to suggest that instead of traveling into the land of Nod as a free man, he was sold off as a slave.

The indication of power, social status or pedigree is not the only reasons why cultural groups used tattoos. Evidence has come forward that suggests that some were applied because they had curative properties. This claim has been made in the case of Ötzi. The majority of his tattoos are arraigned in groups of one, two, three, four and even seven parallel lines that run along the length of his body. Examination by three separate acupuncture societies revealed that the many of the tattoos on Ötzi's body transverse traditional Chinese acupuncture points. The cross-shaped emblems found on his left ankle and knee correspond to acupuncture trigger points.

Nowadays, acupuncture is sought out for the relief of pain, where specific points are activated along channels known as *meridians* (Fig. 70). Fifteen of Ötzi tattoos are located on the bladder meridian. Acupuncturists traditionally target this meridian for the relief of back pain. The crossed tattoo patterns found near his left ankle, in acupuncture texts, is considered the *master point for back pain*. Physical examination of Ötzi body revealed that he suffered from severe knee, hip, ankle and back issues as well as intestinal disorders. The placement of the tattoos on Ötzi body potentially indicates something else: that the concepts associated with the ancient healing tradition of acupuncture were well understood at least 5000 years ago.

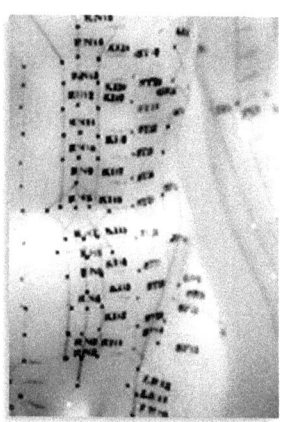

Figure 70 - Acupuncture points of the human body.

Medical treatment is also suggested in the tattoos of a 1000-year-old Peruvian woman who was found in the sands of Chiribaya Alta region of the Southern Peruvian desert. Decorative tattoos of birds, reptiles, and apes, as well as other symbols, cover her body. On the upper part of her back and neck are also a series of different sized circular tattoos in seemingly random positions. Unlike the others that adorn her body, these do not appear to be decorative. This discovery has led researchers to wonder if these tattoos, like Ötzi's, were for medicinal purposes.

Microscopy techniques, carried out by Maria Anna Pabst from the University of Graz in Austria, were used to determine the composition of the tattooing materials. Her findings indicate that soot, a conventional material utilized in ancient tattoos, was used to create the decorative markings. The irregular circular tattoos, on the other hand, were made of partially burned plant material. This led Pabst to believe that the woman may have experienced additional health benefits from the plant matter used. Pabst also points out that the circles found on the woman's neck paralleled the traditional acupuncture points that would be used for relaxation or to relieve neck pain.

Scarification

The practice of scarification or cicatrization parallels that of tattooing. Scarification is a painful and bloody way of permanently marking the skin (Fig. 71). A series of small scars are created by cutting the epidermis on the back, arms, stomach or legs and manipulating the healing process. The skin of individuals, who undergo this procedure, are incised with a sharp instrument such as a knife, piece of glass, a stone or even a coconut shell. Soot or other irritants are rubbed into the open wounds. This process accentuates the scars and makes them even more prominent by producing raised lumps (keloids) that are artfully combined to create a series of complex forms and elegant patterns over large areas of the body.

The process of scarification as a permanent marking system was widely practiced in cultures that have dark skin and was employed where traditional tattoos would not be readily seen. Thus, groups in Africa, Australia, Papua New Guinea and New Zealand commonly followed this practice. Evidence of its use also extends throughout North, Central and South America.

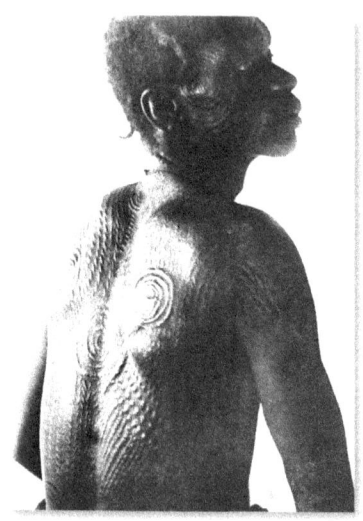

Figure 71 - Scarified back of a man from the Democratic Republic of the Congo.

The earliest suggestive evidence of scarification was found at the archaeological site at Ain Ghazal, in Jordan. Here two Paleolithic figurines, dating back to 8000 BC, display markings that appear to indicate scarification. Rock paintings of human figures discovered in the Tassili n'Ajjer mountain range in the Sahara, which date back to 7000 BC, also show markings consistent with scarification. These finds suggest that this ancient practice had been in use at least 10,000 years ago. In the Americas, stone sculptures created by the Olmec culture found at Villahermosa in Mexico, depict figures whose faces and shoulders show marks that too suggest this practice. These statues date to about 1000 BC.

Scarification, like tattooing, was performed for a variety of reasons. They were used to mark stages of life such as puberty and marriage. They transmitted information about an individual's identity, family, social status and religious role. African art expert, Susan Vogel, notes that in Africa *"Scarification and other forms of body decoration were traditionally considered marks of civilization. They distinguished the civilized, socialized human body from the body in its natural state and from animals."*

The marks of scarification, for some, were perceived as a sign of beauty while for others they represented the enemies they killed in battle. For many, it was a mark of pride or bravery. The discomfort experienced was thought to test their capacity to endure the tasks of adult life. For women, it was a visual testament to their ability to withstand pain, including the pain of childbirth. Thus the more scars a woman had on her body, the higher the bride price.

Individuals who did not submit to this painful process, like those who were left unmarked with a tattoo, would not achieve full standings in their community. They could not get married. They could not hunt. Nor could they participate in activities that were reserved for the adult members of society.

Scarification has also been used to treat illness as part of many traditional healing rituals. The Dogomba, of Northern Ghana, believe that all disease originates in the blood. Indigenous healers would cut the skin and apply a remedy to the wound so that its healing benefits could enter the bloodstream directly. Although miles away, this practice supports the speculation that the 1000-year-old tattooed Peruvian woman received medical treatments. Healing plants were applied to open wounds for health benefits in both cases.

Ear Piercing/Earlobe Stretching

The piercing of the ears, like tattooing, has been practiced all over the world since ancient times. Our good friend Ötzi the Iceman, the 5,300-year-old mummy we discussed earlier, displays our most primitive example of ear piercing and ear stretching. When discovered, Ötzi ears were not only pierced, but his earlobes had been stretch to 2.5-4 inches (7-11mm) in diameter. It must be concluded, even with this early find, that this practice is at least as old as Ötzi, but more likely much older.

In 2004, Chinese archaeologists discovered what they believe to be the oldest pair of earrings in the world. Called a *jue* in old Chinese, these carved ornaments are believed to have been worn as earrings. They were found in the burial of a woman from the Xinglongwa culture of Inner Mongolia that thrived about 7500 and 8200 years ago.

Figure 72 - Kenyan man with ear plugs.

In the Sumerian city of Ur, the home of the Biblical patriarch Abraham, earrings were discovered in royal graves of this ancient Iraqi site that date back to around 2500 BC. They have also been unearthed in Crete and date to approximately 2000 BC. Earrings were also frequently worn during the Eighteenth dynasty in Egypt (1550–1292 BC) where they took the form of a dangling gold hoop.

Ear gauging and ear stretching (Fig. 72) were also body modifications that were used by our ancestors. In many cultures, holes were created by piercing the ear with a thorn, a sharpened twig or a stingray spine. The holes were slowly expanded until the desired size was reached. Small pegs, in some societies, were inserted into the ear holes, which over time were replaced by larger ones. In other cultures, increasingly heavy jewelry or stones were attached to the ear, thus weighing down the ear hole and eventually stretching the earlobes. The wealthy utilized precious metals such as gold or silver to adorn their modified earlobes. The remainder of society employed animal bones, tusks, horns, wood, precious

Chapter 12: Body Modification

stones such as jade or obsidian, shells or attractive rocks to decorate their stretched ears.

Ear piercing, like other body modifications, was often tied to puberty rituals. The size of one's ears holes often indicated the social standing of members of a tribe. In many cultures, the earlobes of both the elites and commoners were pierced and gauged, but the larger the stretching, the more important the individual was to the community. Chiefs, for example, had the most substantial stretching, while the piercings of other members of the tribe varied based on their social status. Stretched piercings have also been used to identify an individual's sexual capability and potency.

Earrings and earplugs were a sign of nobility and wealth for the Tlingit of the Pacific Northwest and an indicator of wealth and beauty for the Egyptians. In eastern Asia, stretched ears indicated wisdom and compassion. This is why, it is conjectured, the Buddha is depicted with long ears. The Buddha, according to legend, had the ability to hear the cries and suffering of the world and through kindness and compassion ease their pain.

Women were both the rulers and responsible for communicating with their gods in the Xinglongwa Culture. They used their jade earrings as a tool to connect with the heavens. When guidance was needed, they believed the jade earrings would help them hear their gods, who assisted them in the decisions making process. Many tribes, in turn, saw ear piercing as a defense against evil spirits. They held that demons could enter into the body through the ear. Ear holes filled with metal earrings were said to repel evil spirits thus preventing it from happening.

> *These kingly jewels assert[ed] the inherent superiority of their wearer within the community of human beings, transforming a person of merely noble rank into a being who can test and control the divine forces of the world.*
> – Stone of Kings: in Search of the Lost Jade of the Maya, Gerard Helferich

The Old Testament of the *Bible* also reflects the concept of communication with the spirit world via the use of earrings.

> *Then God said to Jacob, "Arise, go up to Bethel and live there, and make an altar there to God, who appeared to you when you fled from your brother Esau." So Jacob said to his household and to all who were with him, "Put away the foreign gods which are among you, and purify yourselves and change your garments; and let us arise and go up to Bethel, and I will make an altar there to God, who answered me in the day of my distress and has been with me wherever I have gone." So they gave to Jacob all the foreign gods which they had and the rings which were in their ears, and Jacob hid them under the oak which was near Shechem.*
>
> – Genesis 35: 3-4

Septum & Nose Piercing

The nose is another part of the head that has been pierced since antiquity. Nose piercing was a common practice in the Middle East. Husbands would give their wives nose rings to ensure their financial security. Olden manuscripts and Vedic texts, which are believed to date back 6000 years, mention nose piercing and nose rings. The *Bible* also mentions nose rings. In Genesis 24:22, Isaac, Abraham's son, gives his future wife, Rebekah, a golden *Shanf*, which translates to nose ring in English.

In the holistic health system, Ayurveda, practitioners instruct that the nose is associated with the reproductive organs. Indian women, on the night before her wedding, would have her left nostril pierced. In many cultures, nose rings were

Chapter 12: Body Modification

a mark of great beauty. They indicated a family's wealth and social standing. They also signified an individual's virility, manliness, and power.

The nostril was not the only part of the nose that was pierced. Popular around the world was the custom of septum piercing (Fig. 73), a practice that comes second to ear piercing. Cultures, including many Native American tribes (Aztecs, Mayans, Incas, and Inuit), the tribes of New Guinea, in India, Africa, Pakistan, the Middle East and Australia performed septum piercing.

Figure 73 - Inuit septum piercing.

The nasal septum is the bone and cartilage of the nose that separates the nasal cavity into the two nostrils. The cartilage, in this procedure, is not pierced, but rather the space between the cartilage and the bottom of the nose. An incision in this fleshy area allowed for the insertion of small items. Increasingly larger sticks or stingray spines were introduced into the hole to extend its diameter until it reached the desired gauge (hole size). Decorative materials used included feathers, bones, animal tusks, bits of wood and even the bones of an enemy slain in battle.

Septum piercings symbolized wealth and (among men) virility. Some septum jewelry was so large that it prevented the wearer from being able to eat without lifting the ornament during meals. The Australian aboriginals pierced their septum with the goal of flattening the nose. They believed a flat nose to be the most desirable looking. Interestingly, unlike much of the body modifications covered so far, septum piercing does not appear to be associated with life events such as puberty or marriage.

Labret Piercing / Lip Stretching

Labret piercing and its associated lip stretching are another of the strange and painful body modification that goes back into deep antiquity. A Labret is an ornament worn in a hole that has been pierced through the skin below the lower lip or in the upper lip near the corners of the mouth or cheek. We see remnants of this practice in archaeological finds, as well as in iconographic indications such as in murals, figurines, and stelae. Some of the earliest evidence validating the use of labrets comes from the Sudan, Ethiopia, Mesoamerica, and Ecuador. They date back to 8700 BC, 1500 BC, and 500 BC respectfully.

Figure 74 - Ethiopian woman with lip plate. Image courtesy of Gianfranco Gori.

Labret piercing traditionally took place in early childhood or at the onset of puberty. The initial incision was usually quite small, but large enough to insert a slender object into the hole to prevent it from closing. The piercing, over the course of a lifetime, was periodically stretched to accommodate larger ornaments such as a plug (labret) or a plate. It was not uncommon for women, in some parts of Africa, to stretch their lower lip to such a significant degree that they were able to accommodate a lip plate or lip ring that was up to 6 inches (15cm) in diameter (Fig. 74).

Labrets take on all shapes and sizes. Inlays, incised designs, and attachments were frequent additions to standard labret forms. Some Aztec and Maya nobility wore stunning labrets made out of pure gold. Many were styled to look like serpents or had stones inset in them (Fig. 75). Others wore labret jewelry made out of jade or obsidian. Materials used to fabricate a labret included wood, ivory, precious metals,

Chapter 12: Body Modification

stones, abalone shell, bone, quartz crystals and in the case of lip plates, wood or clay. Because labrets are made of durable materials, a sizable number have been recovered from archeological sites around the world. These finds add to our understanding of them and the far-flung distribution of this practice.

Labrets, like other forms of body modification, were worn for personal adornment and to reflect one's socioeconomic status, social affiliation, and hereditary. High-ranking individuals wore the largest labrets. In some cultures, they were seen as a form of spiritual protection, as an indicator of sexual maturity or as a sign of fertility. If used as part of an initiation ceremony, it reflected the individual's ability to take on adult responsibility and even marry.

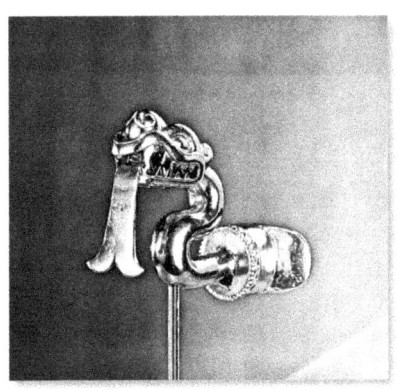

Figure 75 - Gold Aztec labret.

Among the Dogon tribe of Africa, lip piercing has religious significance. Author Anthony Seeger, in his article *The Meaning of Body Ornaments: A Suya Example*, suggests that labrets were coupled with oral productions such as speaking and chanting. The labrets of the indigenous tribes of the North Pacific sometimes took on the form of a mouth with a protruding tongue. The tongue was viewed not as an organ of taste, but as the organ of speech. It demonstrated one's mastery over the spirits that may enter and exit via this entrance. Similarly, it was seen as a sign of wisdom or identified an individual's ability to appease the forces of nature.

Among the Tlingit people of the Pacific North West, a woman who was to have her lip pierced was required to fast before the procedure began. This practice leads one to believe that there may have been a broader ritual significance to this observance. We can only assume that other cultures held similar traditions.

Dental Modifications

The exact purpose of dental modifications remains a mystery, yet people have been mutating their teeth for thousands of years. This practice is widespread and takes on four primary forms: filing, drilling with inlays, ablation (the intentional removal of specific teeth) and staining. This type of body modification crossed social and economic lines where it was used by elites and commoners alike. Dental modifications, like other body modifications, are believed to communicate cultural affiliation, determine physical attractiveness, and indicate social status.

It does seem clear that our Neolithic ancestors had an understanding of how to modify dentition some 8-9,000 years ago. In an archaeological site in Pakistan, eleven teeth from nine different individuals were excavated from a Stone Age graveyard. Several of the teeth showed clear signs of dentistry. *"One individual had three drilled teeth, while another had a tooth that had been drilled twice,"* Roberto Macchiarelli, an anthropology professor at the University of Poitiers, France, said. In another individual, a deep cavity was hollowed out. Microscopic studies revealed that smoothing of the teeth took place, which indicates that the individuals lived well after the procedure was performed and was able to continue chewing with the modified tooth.

In an interesting side note, Macchiarelli goes on to inform us, *"Though the dental manipulation lasted near Mehrgarh for about 1,500 years, the practice completely disappeared with the onset of the metal age about 7,000 years ago. There*

Chapter 12: Body Modification

is no evidence of this procedure in graveyards from much later periods, despite the continuation of poor dental health. We have no idea why it stopped."

Teeth Filing

Tooth filing, or tooth sharpening, takes on many forms. These include filing the ends of the teeth to a point, filing them down to make them flat, or cutting out a portion of the tooth to create a particular shape. The earliest evidence of dental alterations are modified teeth that were found in West Africa. This site dates to about 3000 BC. The oldest example of tooth modification found in the Americas comes from Mexico and dates to 1400 BC.

One of the most straightforward forms of tooth filing is the carving of parallel and crosshatched lines into the visible surfaces of the tooth enamel. Graves ranging from North America, Mesoamerica, Europe, Africa, and Asia all display this type of dental engraving. Skulls uncovered in Viking graves that date from 800 to 1050 AD offer the first historical example of dental modification among Europeans. The dental marks occur in pairs or triplets and were cut deep into the tooth enamel. The find also suggests that the striations were painted with red colored resin and charcoal to produce a decorative effect. It also implies that this form of dental modification may have been ornamental rather than functional.

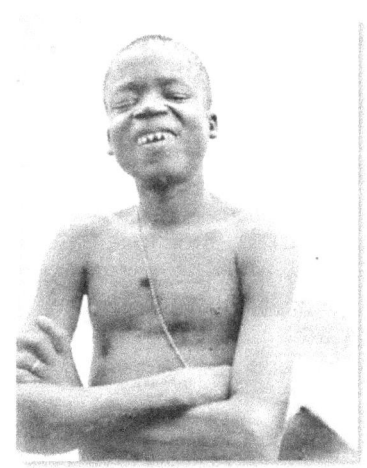

Figure 76 - African boy with filed teeth.

Caroline Arcini, an anthropologist at the National Heritage Board in Lund, Sweden notes: *"The only place I know of [where people] have similar horizontal filing marks on their teeth ... is the area of the Great Lakes in America and the present states of Illinois, Arizona, and Georgia."* Her observation suggests that this form of tooth filing was not isolated to England, Denmark, and Sweden.

Many cultures practice a style of tooth filing in which the teeth are filed to a sharpened point (Fig. 76). In this variety, the teeth are not in actuality filed but are chipped away to create the intended shape. The Indians of the Amazon Valley file their central incisors to points in imitation of the piranha that live in the rivers. The Wapare people of Africa sharpened their teeth to imitate sharks. In Mesoamerica, researchers contend that individuals filed their teeth to emulate their pointed-toothed solar deity. This custom is especially prevalent amongst tribes in West Africa and the Congo and isolated groups in Southeast Asia, including people from the Andaman Islands, Malaysia, Thailand, and the Philippines.

In Indonesia, women filed their teeth to find a husband. On Bali, the opposite occurred. An individual's canines and incisors were filed flat and were an indicator of social, aesthetic and spiritual well-being. They assert that pointed teeth represent anger, jealousy, and other similar negative emotions. By removing the animal-like qualities of the teeth, it would likewise remove the savage aspects of the soul.

Much mystery also surrounds the seemingly expert medical skill used to perform tooth filing. It was done so precisely that no severe damage occurred, in particular, the loss of the modified tooth. The pain involved in transforming the teeth must have been incredible, especially at a time when anesthesia did not exist. As historian Scott Russell notes: *"there is no evidence of the tools or techniques available in accounts or the archeological record to explain how or why this practice emerged."*

Dental Inlays

Inlaying teeth, with precious metals or gemstones, is another form of dental modification. The earliest evidence of a dental inlay date to about 1300 years ago and was found in an ancient Mayan site. Even today, we are hard-pressed to explain the apparent expertise of these early dental practitioners. The holes drilled into the teeth narrowly avoided hitting nerves and exposing pulp. The work was done so precisely that it appears as if no severe damage was done to the tooth. Evidence also suggests that the individual who had this procedure performed still had use of the modified tooth. In his book, *Relación de las Islas Filipinas*, Jesuit chronicler Pedro Chirino explains how in the Tagalog people of the Philippines decorated their teeth with gold inserts.

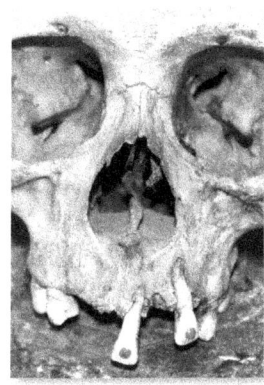

Figure 77 - Mayan skull with dental inlays

They even used to, and do yet, insert gold between their teeth as an ornament... From the edge to the middle of the tooth they neatly bore a hole, which they afterwards fill with gold, so that this drop or point of gold remains as a shining spot in the middle of the black tooth. This seems to them most beautiful ...

– Relación de las Islas Filipinas, Pedro Chirino

The Maya are well known for this form of dental modification. Small holes were commonly pierced into their incisors and canines and were embedded with a variety of minerals of beautiful colors (Fig. 77). Researchers are still mystified. How were they able to so implant jade, obsidian, pyrite, and turquoise so precisely into their teeth? The work done has stood the test of time. Many Mayan skulls, with their inlaid stones still preserved intact in the individual's teeth, have been discovered.

Tooth Ablation

The intentional removal of healthy frontal teeth (tooth ablation) has a long history and appears in a diverse number of cultures around the world. Accidents, facial trauma, congenital maladies, etc. can contribute to traditional tooth loss. There are also several reasons why skeletal remains may lose their teeth. Researchers when investigating cases of tooth ablation focus in on two primary features: the observance of a repetitive pattern of tooth loss in seemingly good teeth and the absence or presence of alveolar bone changes.

Archaeological evidence of this practice appears in Africa, Australia, Europe, Siberia, Japan, Southeast Asia and the Americas. Cultures performed tooth ablation as a rite of passage, to indicate his or her social status or as a sign of mourning. The Japanese *Jomon* culture, who thrived from 13,000 to 2300 years ago, practiced this rite extensively. Anthropologists from the University of Nevada in their article *Jomon Tooth Ablation* note:

> *For the Jomon, life milestones were commemorated by the extraction of different tooth classes. The removal of particular teeth immediately marked your place in society. The various examples display individuals at different places/ranks within society. With a flash of a smile, one would know the individual's family, if they were an adult or not, if they were married, if they had experienced the death of a loved one, or if they had children. There was no need to ask as your body openly displayed your identity.*
>
> – Jomon Tooth Ablation

Chapter 12: Body Modification

Tooth Staining

The final way in which dental modifications have occurred in our past is teeth staining or the staining of the soft tissue surrounding the teeth. Archaeologists, working on the island of Palawan, discovered graves that display the earliest recorded cases of deliberate dental staining. These graves date to about 2600 BC.

The most widely spread variety of tooth staining comes from individuals who chew betel nut. An areca nut, or betel nut, is the seed of the areca palm, which grows in much of the tropical Pacific and parts of east Africa. Chewing a mixture of areca nut and betel leaf constitutes an important cultural activity in many Asian and Oceanic countries. We have already discussed the psychoactive aspect of this plant, but a byproduct of chewing this mixture is the staining of the mouth, teeth, and gums. In betel nut chewing countries, the crimson cheeks and black teeth of betel nut chewing were hallmarks of female beauty. Similarly, the long termed consumption of the psychoactive substance Khat can cause permanent darkening of the teeth. Other indigenous groups utilized small pieces of *lacha* for red staining or used soot from guava trees or the Benguet pine to produce blackened teeth.

In Japan, women, noblemen and samurai warriors practiced the tradition of teeth dyeing for hundreds of years. There are long-standing cultural reasons for tooth blackening in Japan. They believed that only savages, wild animals, and demons had long white teeth. Blackened teeth assured that one would not be mistaken for an evil spirit. Women in Vietnam blackened their teeth through a tooth lacquering process. Blackened teeth indicated that a girl was grown up and ready for marriage. The practice was considered physically attractive and had the added health benefit of preventing dental cavities and gum disease.

Circumcision

Circumcision is a rite that many believe is exclusive to the Judeo-Christian faith. In Genesis 17, God appears to Abram (Abraham) and makes a covenant between him and his people. Abram is instructed to circumcise himself as well as every male member of his household. This practice was to continue throughout his future generations, where all male infants were to be circumcised on the eighth day of life. The observance of the circumcision rite is reiterated in Leviticus 12:3, where we are told: *"On the eighth day the flesh of his foreskin shall be circumcised."* Contrary to the fallacious belief that circumcision is allied with the Judeo-Christian faith, it is one of the oldest and most common surgical procedure performed in both the ancient and modern world.

Circumcision is the deliberate removal of a fold of skin (the prepuce) that covers the head of the un-erect penis. This practice pre-dates recorded history and is believed to have existed before the movement of early modern humans. Günter Wagner, in his book *The Bantu of North Kavirondo* suggests, *"The distribution of circumcision and initiation rites throughout Africa, and the frequent resemblance between details of ceremonial procedure in areas thousands of miles apart, indicate that the circumcision ritual has an old tradition behind it and in its present form is the result of a long process of development."*

The earliest suggestive evidence of circumcision, including foreskin retraction, comes from the Upper Paleolithic period in Europe and goes back to about 30,000 BC. Phallic batons (Fig. 78), carved from polished antlers, stones, and

Figure 78 - Paleolithic phallic batons.

Chapter 12: Body Modification

bones, (Fig. 78) have been recovered from sites primarily in France but have also been found in areas ranging from Spain, through Germany and as far as Ukraine. They appear in a similar geographic area as the Venus figures, such as the Venus of Willendorf and the Venus of Hohle Fels (Fig. 68). In addition to depicting a penis with its foreskin removed, some of these portable phallic art pieces indicate that ritual and decorative cutting, tattooing, and piercing was also being performed on this delicate body part.

The oldest artistic depiction of the ritual act of circumcision comes from the tomb of Ankhmahor (2355-2343 BC) the vizier under the reign of King Teti in ancient Egypt. A bas-relief wall carving found in his vault reveals images of young men as they undergo this procedure (Fig. 79). The examination of male Egyptian mummies also offers concrete evidence that this observance was in use at least 3500 years ago and crossed all levels of ancient Egyptian society. The Greek historian Herodotus, writing in the mid 5th century BC, commented on this custom: "[The Egyptians] *practice circumcision for the sake of cleanliness, considering it better to be cleanly than comely.*" He goes on to state that circumcision was performed by the Colchians, Egyptians, and Ethiopians from time immemorial.

In Australia, during the *Dreamtime*, legend states that two individuals who lived in the western sky introduced circumcision to the Arunta tribe. It was first performed using a fire-stick. In time, the fire-stick was replaced with a stone knife (See sidebar: *Early Customs & Traditions Of The Arunta*). Christopher Columbus, when he arrived in the New World, noted that many of the natives were circumcised. The Dominican friar, Diego Durán, who followed

Figure 79 - Relief of boys being circumcised from tomb of Ankhmahor.

Cortés into the Americas, believed that the Aztecs also practiced this rite. Durán's beliefs have been challenged in recent years. Researchers now think that the incisions made into the prepuce were a part of the Aztec's practice of ritual bloodletting and not the act of circumcision itself.

The reasons offered as to why circumcision originated are extensive. Circumcision, according to a variety of scholars, began as:

- A religious sacrifice.
- A rite of passage marking a boy's entrance into adulthood.
- A form of sympathetic magic to ensure virility or fertility.
- An aid to hygiene.
- A means of discouraging masturbation.
- A way of marking those of higher social status.
- A way of distinguishing one group from their neighbors.
- A way of increasing a man's attractiveness to women.
- A selective advantage in deferring reproduction until after puberty.
- A means of reducing sexual pleasure.
- A means of humiliating enemies and slaves.
- A way to demonstrate one's ability to endure pain.
- A male counterpart to menstruation.
- A way to repel demons.
- A way to treat a medical condition known as phimosis, which offered advantages to tribes that practiced it.

In their article, *Why Circumcision: From Prehistory to the Twenty-First Century*, Guy Cox and Brian Morris propose that the knowledge and practice of circumcision existed in every culture on Earth since Paleolithic times. They argue that cultures who do not currently practice this rite stopped it in more recent times (historical time) versus having never adopted it in the first place. They go on to suggest, "*The most likely explanation is that at a time of extreme privation, perhaps during a glacial period, ritual life was lost in the struggle for survival."*

Subincision

Similar to circumcision, abet seemingly much more extreme and painful, is the practice of subincision. Subincision involves the cutting of a slit down the length of the penis into the urethra. The urethra is the long tube that runs through the penis and allows urine to pass out of the body. The incision can be of varying lengths. Initially, an inch long slit is cut into the underside of the penis, which over time is extended until the entire urethra is converted into an open channel. Subincision can affect a man's ability to urinate causing him to have to sit or squat while relieving himself. It is suggested that it improves a man's sexual performance, but can, in the same breath, impede his ability to impregnate women.

The practice of subincision, most notably associated with Australia, is found around the world where it is used to identify a man who holds a position of status within the tribe. In some cultures, the site used for ritual bloodletting was the subincised penis. Samburu boys, according to Edward Margetts, in his article entitled *Sub-incision Of The Urethra In The Samburu Of Kenya*, shares a rare report of young boys, before they are circumcised, carrying out this procedure on themselves while cattle herding.

Early Customs & Traditions Of The Arunta

We have hitherto spoken of the Alcheringa in general terms, using the word to denote the whole period during which the mythical ancestors of the present Arunta tribe existed. In reality the traditions of the tribe recognize four more or less distinct periods in the Alcheringa. We have:—

(1.) A period during which two individuals who lived in the western sky, and were called Ungambikula, came down to earth and transformed Inapertwa creatures into human beings whose totem names were naturally those of the animals or plants out of which they were transformed. The Ungambikula also performed the rite of circumcision on certain, but not all, of the men, using for this purpose a fire-stick.

(2.) A period during which the Ullakupera or little hawk men introduced the use of the stone knife during circumcision. In addition they carried on the work commenced by the Ungambikula of transforming Inapertwa creatures into human beings, and further still, they introduced the class names now in use, viz. Panunga, Purula, Bulthara, Kumara. We may presume that along with the introduction of the class names there was instituted in connection with them some system of marriage regulations, but what exactly this was, there is not sufficient evidence to show.

(3.) A period, following closely upon the latter, during which the Achilpa or wild cat men introduced the rite of Ariltha or sub-incision. It is said of the Achilpa, also, that they arranged the initiation ceremonies in their proper order, first circumcision, then sub-incision, and lastly the Engwura.

(4.) A period during which, first of all, the marriage system was changed owing to the influence of certain Erlia or emu people, with the result that Purula men might marry Panunga women, Bulthara men Kumara women, and vice versa. Secondly, and at a later period, each of these classes was divided into two, so that, to a Panunga man, for example, only half of the Purula women were eligible as wives, the other half being Unkulla or forbidden to him.

-- The Native Tribes of Central Australia
Baldwin Spencer and F.J. Gillen

Chapter 12: Body Modification

Cranial Deformation

Cranial deformation is another distinct, ancient and painful tradition. The objective of cranial deformation is to modify the shape of the head by elongating it. This procedure, once performed, cannot be reversed and individuals who have it done, unlike tattooing and circumcision, cannot conceal it. It is a permanent visible marker that has been used to identify a cultural group and select individuals within a society.

Cranial deformation is a long and arduous process that begins shortly after birth. When a child is born, the infants head is fashioned or molded into a uniquely long and slender shape. A caregiver, in the simplest method employed, would put pressure on, or gently massage the child's head daily until they achieved the desired shape. The second approach constrains the child's head in a mechanical device which, over time, produced the desired elongated shape (Fig. 80). Unlike other body modification, this type of ornamentation always commenced during infancy. It is only during infancy that the cranial bones are still tender, and pliable and the sutures between the bones are unfixed which allows for the shaping or reshaping of the head.

Skulls displaying clear signs of cranial deformation surfaced in the archeological record of the Neolithic Era starting around 10,000 BC. Some of the earliest examples of elongated skulls

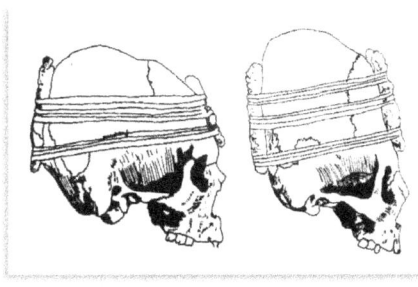

Figure 80 – Tabular cranial deformation apparatus. Image courtesy of Jean Pezzali.

were discovered in south-eastern Australia in *Coobool Creek* and *Kow Swamp*. Remarkably, modified craniums found in the *Shanidar Cave* in Iraq date to about the same time. In the eastern highlands of Brazil, another specimen recovered from *Confins Cave* dates to about 7566 BC.

Starting around 5000 BC, the tradition of skull modification appears to have expanded. This assumption is based upon the increased number of remains with elongated skulls recovered. Some researchers believe that the convention of cranial manipulation mushroomed as early hunter-gather societies began to coalesce into urban environments. Figurines with deformed crania start to appear in the archeological record further supporting the antiquity and distribution of this custom.

The tradition of cranial deformation is often associated with ancient and indigenous cultures and not with contemporary ones. One might assume if it were practiced in the west, it would have occurred sometime in our remote past and was abandoned by civilized society. This assumption is far from the case. Researchers, such as neurologist and psychiatrist Achille Foville, documented the practice of cranial deformation in France. Surveying the crania of inmates at a French public asylum, he evaluated 431 individuals at the facility. His findings revealed a remarkable 50% of the population with clear signs of deformation, with some of them being considered severe in his estimation.

Figure 81 – Painting depicting Flathead Indian tabular cranial deformation method.

There are two primary forms of artificial cranial deformation - tabular and circumferential. Tabular cranial modifications involve the compression of the front or front and back of the child's skull by cradle boarding or other cephalic apparatus (Fig. 81). It is the most prominent type of deformation found around the world and includes unintentional, yet unnatural, variations to the cranium. After birth, a board is placed on the child's head and is bound in place, which ultimately flattens the child's forehead.

If a child's head is placed between two boards, one in the front and one in the back, and then bound, the compression results in an even more exaggerated and distinctive head shape. This type of modification causes the skull to expand laterally and superiorly. Garcilaso de la Vega writing in 1609 described the methods used by the inhabitants of specific regions of Peru. He states: *"From birth they pressed their children's skull between two planks tied together at the ends, which they tightened a little every day... After three years, a child's skull was deformed for life, so they removed the apparatus."*

Head modification utilizing the tabular method can occur unintentionally as a side effect of childcare practices. Circumferential modifications, on the other hand, are unquestionably produced by design. Constricting bandages are wrapped like a tight ring around the child's skull forcing its growth upright. This method reduces the diameter of the skull while pushing the cranium upward and backward. Tight fitting caps or bonnets worn by infants often produced an elongated appearance to the head. Constricting bands, up to three in number, were also used to create a conical head form. Evidence, based upon skulls discovered, suggests that as additional bands were applied to the head a more exaggerated shape was produced.

Surveys of cranial deformation around the world have also unveiled one other remarkable fact. If the tradition of cranial deformation had originated in one location and then spread across the globe, as researchers suggest, then one would expect to find large geographic areas in which tabular head shaping methods were uniquely employed and then others that utilized the circular method. An example of this would be the discovery of only tabular modifications in South and Mesoamerica and circumferential style modifications in Egypt and the Levant.

What we find are many instances where both types are being utilized within relatively close proximity to one another.

In the Aymara culture of the highland area near Tiwanaku, Brazil, for example, the predominant practice was of circumferential compression. In the coastal regions of Peru, at the same time, tabular deformations were prevalent. Even in the island nations of Oceania, circular modifications have been found in countries such as Malekula and New Hebrides, while tabular modifications were practiced on the neighboring Solomon Islands and New Caledonia.

They have also discovered that the methods, customs, and traditions used appear the most intense in specific geographic areas and deteriorate as one moves away from this focal point until finally the practice is no longer performed. This dispersion suggests that this rite was established in chief cultural centers and then spread into the surrounding areas.

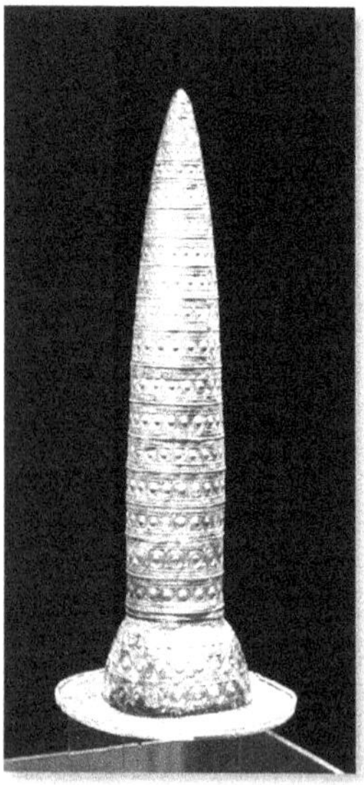

Many cultures also employed measures to accentuate this modified form. The hair was pulled back and braided or put into a bun or topknot to further exaggerate the elongated shape of the head. Pointed hats, such as the ones worn by many of the Egyptian pharaohs, are believed to be apparel used to embellish head shape. Only the nobility, in Egypt, were allowed to wear tall pointed hats. They symbolized their elevated status.

The donning of pointed hats was not limited to Egyptian royalty. Several conical brimless extremely long gold hats, extending as high as 35 inches (85 cm), have been discovered in central Europe with the earliest one dating to about 1400 BC (Fig. 82). These obviously were not to be worn by the

Figure 82 – Solid gold European pointed hat. Image courtacy of Philip Pikart.

Chapter 12: Body Modification

common man. In ancient Greece, slaves who were released from bondage were allowed to wear a pointed hat called a *pileus*. Did this indicate their increased social status? Early art also shows image after image of individuals wearing pointed hats. Were they emulating this ancient tradition of cranial deformation with their clothing? Even today, the guest of honor at a birthday party will put on a pointed hat to symbolize his or her importance.

The original meaning or ritual significance of this practice has effectively been lost. In the few traces of beliefs that have survived, we find a consistent and general theme, which may reveal at least in part some our ancestor's underlying motivations.

Some cultures report that the practice of cranial deformation was passed on as an edict from the gods. Ancient Polynesian tradition informs us that this right was brought to them by a group of light-skinned people whose home was in the sky. In Central America, claims are made that this custom was employed because the gods told their ancestors to do it. They go on to state that the practice makes it easier to carry burdens. In Peru, the god Manco Cápac ordered the people to perform this strange ritual so that their children would be weak, submissive and obedient. Many cultures think that an elongated head indicates increased intelligence. It is also said to enhance one's beauty or was a trait to be admired. Some cultures believe it will make them look fierce in battle.

A correlation between deformation and the appearance of social classes has also emerged. A deformed head was an indicator of increased social position in many cultures. Extending throughout Europe, a large number of elongated skulls have been discovered in ancient tombs. The elaborate burials they were found in suggest that the interred individuals were of an elite class. Parallel finds have been unearthed in Peru. Some of the most ill-shaped heads were discovered in some of the largest and finest tombs side-by-side with skulls of average size and proportion. A chief or members of the royal family, for example, may exhibit increased deformation, while a priest, shaman or individuals with local eminence may display a less intense modification. Thus, he who has the longest head was the most noble.

Studies into indigenous cultures like the Native American Chinooks of the Pacific Northwest relay that slaves were never permitted to practice this ritual. The ancient Macrocephali people of Africa, of whom the word *macrocephalic* is derived, believed that men of low birth had no right to observe this custom. This regulation may explain in part why all members of a community did not equally employ this modification.

It is unclear why the intentional manipulation of the skull was adopted. This practice once decided upon, takes years to unfold and starts well before a child is grown and enters into a position of power or prestige. It seems evident that this painful procedure was not a response to some innate primal impulse. It also seems hard to fathom that a parent or caregiver would want to inflict years of relentless pain and discomfort on an infant based on an ancient fashion trend. Implementation of elongation requires long termed planning and commitment on the part of the caregiver for it to flourish within a community. Yet, it seems evident that this tradition was so important to our ancestors that it lingered on into the modern era.

Initiation Rites

Why do body modification? Where did we come up with this idea? Were we sitting around a campfire and then out of the blue decide to mutilate ourselves? Body modification is a counter-intuitive act. Why would anyone deliberately disfigure themselves or expose themselves to something so painful and risky? Joseph Campbell noted in his book *Primitive Mythology: The Masks of God* that the rituals of transformation from infancy to manhood were often excruciating ordeals. They held profound religious and spiritual significance for them. The pain and discomfort associated with these rites were bravely endured and were proudly worn from that day forward (Fig. 83).

Was the notion of modifying the body an invention of our ancestors? French naturalist, Jean Louis Armand de Quatrefages de Bréau, writing in 1889, did not think so and found it difficult to accept that these practices originated independently. He pointed to the extraordinary similarities; the uniformity of the methodology, tools and techniques used by cultures around the world and concluded that these practices could not have come about as a natural impulse of the human race.

If the painful traditions associated with body modification were imposed upon humanity, who required it? Could it have been, as we have seen time and time again, the gods? If so, what was their motivation? Peter Markman and Roberta Markman, in their book *Masks of the Spirit: Image and Metaphor in Mesoamerica* suggest that body modifications were a natural but permanent form of the ritual mask and body painting.

Masks and body paint, as you may recall, were used to transform the wearer from animal to man, from man to god impersonator or even a god himself. Why would that be important?

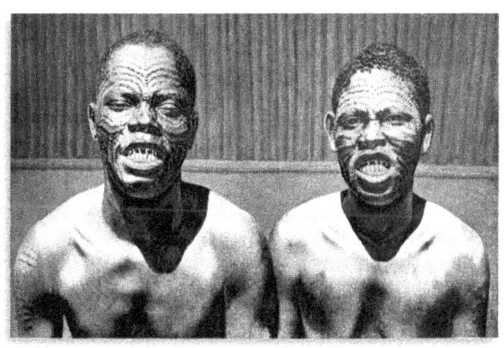

Figure 83 - Young African boys with dental modifications and scarification

According to Steven and Even Strong, authors of *Out Of Australia*, body modification were always tied to initiation rites, which included the receiving of secret knowledge. Each time the body was poked, pinched, cut or prodded, the initiate was taken deeper into the sacred mysteries of the universe.

> *To earn their right to learn secret business, men and woman among the First Australians undertook a huge array of extremely trying physical tests and deprivations. They had to complete their esoteric rite of passage through fortitude and the ability to conquer considerable pain... Once a young Original apprentice successfully copes with his first cut, whether circumcision, tooth avulsion, scarification, etc, some knowledge is shared and a few simple sacred truths are spoken of, but much more is hidden and will remain so until the seeker can pass further tests and take more cuts.*
>
> *– Out Of Australia*, Steven and Even Strong

We see a similar system of degrees and initiation levels in organizations such as the Freemasons, the Rosicrucians, and the Skull and Bones. David V. Barrett, author of *Secret Societies: From the Ancient and Arcane to the Modern and Clandestine*, defines a secret society as any group that possesses the following characteristics: It has carefully graded and progressed teachings. The teachings are available only to selected individuals. The instructions lead to hidden truths and knowledge that bring personal benefits beyond the reach and understanding of the uninitiated. Barrett goes on to say, *"a further characteristic common to most of them is the practice of rituals which non-members are not permitted to observe, or even to know the existence of."* The only difference between traditional cultures and

Figure 84 - Prince Edward VIII in his Mason's regalia. Image courtesy of The Lost Gallery.

Chapter 12: Body Modification

modern secret societies is that secret handshakes, pins, metals and other kinds of regalia, which display their clan affiliation and status within the group, replaced the physical transformation found in the earlier (Fig. 84).

This transition from body modifications to other symbols of office emanate from Abrahamic roots, which deems marking the body a corruption of the *perfect* human form. Sunni Muslims expressly forbid tattooing and believe it is a sin because it involves changing the creation of God. In the Old Testament, we find the passage, *"Ye shall not make any cuttings in your flesh for the dead, nor print any marks upon you: I am the LORD."* - Leviticus 19:28.

Body modifications were replaced with the use of ceremonial dress. Aaron and his sons, in their role as priests, were required to wear specific regalia when entering God's sacrosanct area, the tabernacle of the congregation.

And these are *the garments which they shall make; a breastplate, and an ephod, and a robe, and a broidered coat, a mitre, and a girdle: and they shall make holy garments for Aaron thy brother, and his sons, that he may minister unto me in the priest's office.*

- Exodus 28:4

They shall be worn by Aaron and by his sons when they enter the Tent of Meeting or when they approach the altar to serve in the Holy, so they will not bear iniquity and die. It shall be a perpetual statute for him and for his descendants after him.

– Exodus 28: 43

Today, we have a variety of systems, which provide specifically authorized individuals safe access to a building, secure location, and even computer files while keeping other people out. They can range from computer passwords, electronic keypads, key cards, retinal scans, and other biometric devices. Was the combination of body modifications a kind cataloging system the gods could use so they could quickly identify specific individuals? Were these self-applied markings similar to ear tags or brands that are used in ranching communities today? If body modifications were used as a mnemonic device by the gods, could they, as cultures changed, evolved and progressed, have lost their original significance and become primarily associated with power and prestige?

Chapter 13:
And It Doesn't End There

So far, we have explored a sizeable number of customs and traditions, which are observed on every continent on the planet. These, however, are not the only practices that come from deep antiquity that are unexplainable. Cultures have been practicing medicine far longer than we have written records. Some of their early practices were tied to the ritual experience and included dental modifications and circumcision. Their medical prowess, however, was not limited to these ancient rites. Their skills in the healing arts also included the remediation of disease.

Illness, according to these traditions, was caused by a combination of natural and supernatural causes. If you tripped and broke your leg, were attacked by a wild animal, were injured during a battle or in childbirth, your illness could have come from a *natural* cause. If, on the other hand, you developed a bladder condition, a stomach issue, have chronic diarrhea or abdominal pain, an ancestor, ghost or vengeful god could be blamed for the infirmity.

Every religious tenet has the notion that the essence of man can be either pure or tainted. These unclean states are not observable from the outside. It is, nevertheless, believed that over time the effects of an individual's polluted inner landscape would make itself known. If someone breaks a taboo, secretly or not, the person does not go scot-free. A punishment would ensue. The first indication may appear in the individual's physical or emotional disposition. They may experience a challenge in their life. If the impurity is not addressed, and especially if more taboos are broken, the hardships encountered may escalate into full-blown disasters, which could affect them or influence the entire community. Thus, while a headache is often attributed to stress, high blood pressure or even a brain tumor today, traditional cultures may point to a malevolent spirit entering the head as the cause of their pain and discomfort.

Philip A. Clarke, in his book *Aboriginal People And Their Plants*, states "*In all human cultures, the manner in which sickness is dealt with is shaped by entrenched cultural beliefs and traditions.*" Contemporary researchers suggest that the placebo effect was the cause of the successful healing experienced by early medical practitioners. A placebo is a substance or treatment with no active therapeutic effect. It is mind over matter. People regain their health because they believe the pill or therapy is healing their woes.

Western medicine, nonetheless, has recently begun to appreciate how stress in its various forms can cause ill health a concept that was well-understood in indigenous cultures. They recognized the effect our emotional health plays upon our physical wellbeing and understood that psychological healing was as crucial as physical healing.

> *Aboriginal people believe that if you have an unhappy relationship at home with one person, you are unwell. This can lead to your immune system being sufficiently stress for you to need medical help. In modern Western medicine, drugs might be used to boost your immune system, but from the Aboriginal perspective, you would continue to be sick as long as you had the problem relationship at home.*
>
> – Prehistoric and Egyptian Medicine, Ian Dawson

Chapter 13: And It Doesn't End There

A shaman or medicine man was responsible for maintaining the health of their clan or tribe and was the individual who would be consulted for medical advice (Fig. 85). These healers, like a contemporary *medical intuitive*, evaluated disease. They could look into the body of their patients and see their illnesses. Their assessments, not only examined their patient's physical wellbeing but their mental, emotional and spiritual health as well.

Figure 85 - Native American shaman.

Records indicate that in Mesopotamia when an individual fell ill, there were several types of doctors that could be consulted. There was the *baru* who would make a prognosis based upon omens and through the use of divination. The community's *ashipu* would identify which evil spirits were plaguing them or determine which god was offended thus bringing about the malady. Finally, there was the *asu* who would recommend herbal remedies, treat wounds or perform surgery. It appears by the time of Hammurabi our understanding of the healing arts was well developed and codified.

The practices of asu physicians and their more religious counterparts were so widespread and commonplace that their services and fees were regulated by law: the Code of Hammurabi states that medical fees were on a sliding scale dependent on one's social class (awelum were elites, mushkenum were commoners, and wardum were slaves), that the Babylonian government had the right to inspect a physician's work, and that errors of omission or commission were corporally punishable, among other detailed rules...

...Majno is careful to point out that surgical treatments were definitely subject to the laws set down by Hammurabi, but other medical treatments such as prescriptions or healing rituals were never mentioned in the Code. This is a reflection of the Mesopotamian conception of disease causation: if someone became ill with something other than a wound, it was because of divine retaliation for a personal transgression or the fault of supernatural influences, and therefore the bad outcome of a treatment could not be considered the asu's fault. However, wounds had a visible and unmistakably mundane cause, and therefore a physician should be able to treat it with mundane means like a scalpel; if the physician only worsened the wound, it was considered just as blame-worthy as the perpetration of the original injury.

– Medicine and Doctoring in Ancient Mesopotamia, Emily K. Teall

Our knowledge of traditional healing methods comes into full view when we evaluate the medical know-how of the ancient Egyptians. The renown of Egyptian physicians was recognized all over the ancient world. Papyrus texts indicate that they had remedies for illnesses of the bones, the teeth, for treating the blood, nausea, ulcers, the heart, lungs, urinary tract, inflammation of the joints and many more. A vast number of early medical texts come from this region. The oldest medical treatise of any kind, the *Kahun Gynaecological Papyrus*, dates to 1800 BC and deals primarily with women's health issues, from disease to fertility, pregnancy, and contraception.

Figure 86 - The Edwin Smith Papyrus.

Chapter 13: And It Doesn't End There

The *Edwin Smith Papyrus* (Fig. 86), a virtual textbook on surgery, documents the examination, diagnosis, treatment, and prognosis of numerous ailments. It was written around 1600 BC and is believed to be a copy of several earlier manuscripts. Another early text, the 110-page scroll, the *Ebers Papyrus* (1550 BC) is full of incantations meant to ward off disease-causing demons and includes some 700 magical formulas and remedies. The papyrus contains chapters on intestinal disease and parasites, eye and skin problems, arthritis, bone-setting, diabetes mellitus, contraception, dentistry and the surgical treatment of abscesses and tumors.

The foundation of health practices of early and indigenous cultures around the world, although perhaps less refined and far less documented than those of the ancient Egyptians, follow a similar and consistent theme. The necessity of cleansing the body to eliminate negative humors was well understood. Treatments such as sweating, as we see today in contemporary saunas, were utilized to purify the body of toxic elements and boost the immune system. Hot baths were employed to calm the nervous system, stimulate blood circulation and help relieve everyday aches and pains.

Herbal remedies also featured prominently in these cultures. Preparations were often recommended such as tonics, washes and even aromatherapies. Medicinal clays, such as bentonite, montmorillonite and Fuller's earth were used for their anti-inflammatory, antiseptic, and general cleansing properties. Women would often consume clay for their high mineral content, including calcium, iron, copper, and magnesium especially when pregnant. The importance of a healthy diet was also recognized and many incorporated techniques such as massage and color therapy into their healing practice.

Spells, charms or amulets would be prescribed to expel an evil spirit if supernatural causes were suspected. The shaman might initiate a healing ceremony over the patient. These rites, like the rituals tied to the ecstatic experience, would be filled with prayers, drumming, chanting, toning, meditation, ritual cleansing, the use of directed intention and magic formulas.

Communication with the offended spirit or vengeful god may be employed to restore an individual's health. The spirit world may also be consulted to obtain much-needed guidance in healing the sick person. Arrernte elder, Veronica Perrurle Dobson explains: *"The healer cures the sick person by getting the sick person's spirit and placing it back into their body, making them well again."*

Medicinal Plants

Figure 87 - Herbal remedy.

Plant materials, in the form of herbal medicine, have always been turned to as a cure for diseases and the alleviation of pain. It has been instrumental in supporting vitality and for providing many life-enhancing benefits. Herbal medicine refers to herbs, herbal materials, herbal preparations and finished herbal products that contain the seeds, berries, roots, leaves, fruits, bark, flowers, or even the whole plants as active ingredients. Their use is as old as mankind itself (Fig. 87).

Direct evidence for the use of plants for healing purposes is rare. Like tattooing, plant remains are less likely to survive in the archaeological record. Suggestive evidence for the use of herbs as a tool of healing was first discovered in 1960 by archeologist Ralph Solecki. In a cave in North-Eastern Iraq, his team unearthed a 35–45-year-old adult *Neanderthal* male. His body was found about fifteen meters from the mouth of *Shanidar Cave*. The find indicates that the man was

Chapter 13: And It Doesn't End There

intentionally buried. He was interred in a shallow grave, and his body was placed in a fetal position. Beneath his body was a bed of woven woody horsetail. Surrounding his body was the pollen of many medicinal plants used by modern herbalists including Yarrow, Cornflower, Bachelor's Button, Ragwort, Groundsel, Grape Hyacinth, and St. Barnaby's Thistle.

These plants are reported to have curative powers that include diuretics, astringents and stimulants and ones with anti-inflammatory properties. The arraignment of the pollen grains tells us that the man was buried in the late spring or early summer because the pollen-producing flowers were in bloom. Solecki goes on to suggest that this *Neanderthal* man *"was not only a very important man, a leader, but also may have been a kind of medicine man or shaman in his group."* If this man was indeed an early physician, as the evidence seems to indicate, the knowledge and use of herbs for their therapeutic properties must extend back even further in time than his 60,000-year burial date.

A new study of skeletal remains from *El Sidrón Cave*, a cave in northern Spain may shed even more light on the use of therapeutic herbs. Researchers have detected chemical, and food traces on the teeth of five *Neanderthals* from tiny food fragments in their ancient dental calculus (tartar). Tartar extracted from the 50,000-year-old teeth revealed microscopic plant starch granules, which include traces of the plants *yarrow* and *chamomile*. Chamomile is well known as a treatment for digestive disorders, nerves, and stress, while yarrow works as an antiseptic and is used to treat colds and fevers. Their bitter taste and lack of nutritional value suggest that they were likely chosen and ingested for their medicinal properties rather than as a food source.

One case was particularly intriguing in the find at El Sidrón. Found were the skeletal remains of a teenage boy with a large dental abscess. Analysis of his dental plaque uncovered that he had a parasite in his system that produced chronic diarrhea. The study revealed that he chewed on *poplar*, a tree, which contains *salicylic acid*. Salicylic acid is the active ingredient in aspirin, which is consumed for its analgesic (painkilling) and anti-inflammatory properties. There was also trace evidence of the natural antibiotic mold *Penicillium* (penicillin). What makes this find particularly exciting is the fact that the Penicillium was only found in the dental calculus of the sick teenager and not in the tartar recovered from any of the other individuals. This find is being described as the first real, tangible evidence of *Neanderthals* ingested medicinal plants. This discovery places the practice of herbal medicine to minimally 50,000 years in our past.

Evidence of the use of healing herbs has also been found in the New World. Discovered in a peat bog in Chile were the remains of 16 plants. This early human settlement dates from 14,800 BC to possibly 33,000 BC. The use of medicinal plants is suggested at this location, according to archaeologist Tom Dillehay because only the therapeutic parts of the plants, the roots, and leaves, were present.

> *The isolated hut had a wishbone-shaped foundation made of gravel and hardened sand. Recovered from inside the hut were masticated leaves of boldo, juncus and seawead, all having medicinal properties. Scattered aound the hut were wood, wooden artifacts, stone tools, bones of seven mastodons, and other varities of possibly used medicinal plants, all associated with fire hearths and food pits. This evidence suggest that the wishbone structure was the place of specialized activities, such as hide and meat processings, tool manufacture, and possibly medicinal practices.*
> – The Oxford Companion to Archaeology, Volume 1, Neil Asher Silberman & Alexander A. Bauer

The last bit of subjective evidence comes from the mythological tales from Sumner. The Sumerian epic narrative *Enki and Ninhursag* contains what is believed to be the first written reference to medicinal plants. In it, Enki tastes a variety of vegetation and according to scholars, determines the healing properties they contain.

Chapter 13: And It Doesn't End There

One day, Enki and Isimud were able to see these new plants up there from the marsh. Enki said to Isimud, "I have not determined the destiny of these plants. What is that one? What is that one?"

His minister Isimud had the answers for him. Pointing at the closest one, Isimud replied, "My master, this is a tree-plant." Isimud then proceeded to cut off a piece of the tree-plant and passed it on to Enki, who immediately ate it.

The taste of the tree-plant fuelled even more Enki's desire to know the nature of the other seven plants left. He asked Isimud about the nature of the seven remaining plants.

"My master, this is the honey plant," he said. Isimud pulled it up for him and Enki ate it.

"My master, this is the vegetable plant," Enki said to Isimud, who cut it off for him, and Enki ate it.

"My master, this is the alfalfa grass," he said to him, who pulled it up for him, and Enki ate it.

"My master, this is the atutu plant," he said to him, who cut it off for him, and Enki ate it.

"My master, this is the actaltal plant," he said to him, who pulled it up for him, and Enki ate it.

"My master, this is the [du] plant," he said to him, who cut it off for him, and Enki ate it.

"My master, this is the amharu plant," he said to him, who pulled it up for him, and Enki ate it.

Enki then determined the destiny of the plants. He had them know it in their hearts.

– Enki and Ninhursag

We also find the oldest written evidence for the use of herbs as agents of healing coming from the Sumerians. On a 5000-year-old tablet that was unearthed in Nagpur are 12 recipes for drug preparation, which refer to over 250 different plants. The plants included poppy, laurel, caraway, and thyme, henbane, and Mandrake. The Chinese *Classic of Herbal Medicine (Shennong Bencaojing)*, attributed to the mythical Chinese sovereign Shennong, who is believed to have lived around 2800 BC, is the oldest known list of medicinal herbs. It is said to have been made up of three volumes containing 365 medicines derived from minerals, plants, and animals. Included in this text were also descriptions of their healing properties. Shennong, like Enki, is said to have tasted hundreds of herbs to test their medicinal value.

Herbal medicine is only an example of ancient non-evasive healing techniques. The list of methodologies they employed is extensive and included aromatherapy, chromotherapy, sweat baths, music, toning, energy healing, and exorcism. While we can only speculate when we began to utilize these and other techniques to restore health, in the end, it is easy to see that they have been in use for eons.

Trepanation

The use of herbs or other healing modalities could be seen as a natural step in our social evolution. However, the first documented surgery performed in the world takes medicine to an entirely new level. The procedure was an early form of brain surgery called *trepanation*. Trepanation is used to treat health problems related to intracranial diseases. It involves removing part of the bony structure that surrounds the brain, the cranium. The word trepanation comes from the Greek word *trypanon*, which means *a bore*. The practice of trepanation involves drilling or scraping a hole into the skull to expose the thick membrane that surrounds the brain called the dura mater. The dura mater is a layer of tissue that separated the

Chapter 13: And It Doesn't End There

skull and the brain. Its function is to protect the brain from mechanical injury.

In today's popular culture, many people believe that trepanation was only practiced in Peru, the home of some of the most remarkable examples of cranial deformation found in the world. Scholars are astounded by the surgical prowess of our Peruvian ancestors, yet thousands of skulls have been recovered from around the world that show clear signs of trepanation. This ancient practice was employed all over Europe and Russia, in Africa, Polynesia, China and in South America. It is still performed today in some indigenous cultures.

The study of trepanation finds its roots in France. The year was 1685 when French Benedictine monk Bernard de Montfaucheon discovered a skull with a hole drilled into it. His discovery was initially overlooked by the scientific community of the day until Alexander Francois Barbie du Bovage unearthed a second skull at Nogentles-Les-Vierges in 1816. Examination of this skull revealed that the hole was not the result of head trauma due to an accident, injury or battle but was performed intentionally on this individual. What amazed researchers, who started investigating instances of trepanation beginning in the mid-1800's, was that this procedure was performed on living people and in most cases they survived the surgery.

Explorations into ancient sites around France revealed hundreds of skulls with the tell-tale signs of trepanation. Skulls discovered in the Cavern de l'Homme-Mort, the Sepulchral Grottoes of Baye and in the dolmen of Lozère all date back to the Neolithic era some 8500 years ago. Found at one burial site in France were 120 prehistoric skulls, 40 of which had trepanation performed on them.

The holes that were bored into some of the earliest trepanned skulls were made by scraping away the cranial bone using a sharp stone such as a flake of obsidian or flint. The holes in these skulls vary in size from a few centimeters in diameter to encompassing nearly half of the head.

Evidence of one of the most remarkable ancient brain surgeries was discovered in a burial in Ensisheim, France (Fig. 88). This skull dates to around 5100-4900 BC. What makes this find so fascinating is not that this is one of the oldest skull unearthed, but the fact that the interred man did not *go under the knife* once, but twice. The skeletal material removed from the front of his head measures a massive 2.6 by 2.4 inches (6.4 by 6.0 cm). The other surgical site revealed an even more substantial amount of bone matter missing. This hole measured an enormous 3.7 by 3.6 inch (9.4 by 9.1 cm) in size. Evidence also indicates that the man survived both surgeries because bone healing is evident in each of the holes.

Figure 88 - Edinburgh Skull
Image courtesy of Wellcome Library, London

More than 80% of all individuals who received trepanation during the Neolithic lived months if not years after the procedure. This fact is evidenced by the amount of healing that occurred around the incision site. In Individuals, who die immediately or shortly after surgery, signs of healing are absent, yet many of the skulls display calcium deposits in and around the surgical site. New bone growth is a clear indicator that the individual survived the procedure. Healing calcifications had remarkably sealed the trepanned hole entirely in a few of the skulls examined.

This success rate is unmatched if you compare the results of this procedure to the surgical outcomes of the 18th and 19th centuries. Individuals who received trepanation as a life-giving measure suffered an almost 100% mortality rate. Infections along the surgical site, due to unsanitary conditions, would often lead to sepsis and ultimately death.

We still marvel at the medical skills of our ancestors. How medicine men in indigenous cultures could have such high survival rates is still a mystery in modern medical circles. Their

Chapter 13: And It Doesn't End There

outstanding success rate is a testament to their technical abilities. In their first venture into the realm of medicine, they could effectively complete complicated surgical procedures that modern medicine shies away from. What makes all of their achievements even more incredible is that they were all done in a non-sterile environment, without anesthesia, antiseptics, and antibiotics. The evidence provided by hundreds of remains readily demonstrates their extraordinary achievement – their patients lived to talk about it.

Chapter 14:
More Questions Than Answers

There are things in this world that can be directly observed and measured. This recorded data is a fact. The sun is 92.96 million miles away from the Earth. It rises in the east and sets in the west. Yet, many things are presented to us as being factual, when they are not. They are just theories, the opinion of one or a small group of people that have been accepted as truth by the masses.

It was understood not that long ago, that the world was flat and stars observed in the night sky orbited around the Earth. According to mainstream society of the time, their geocentric belief about the universe was a tried and true fact. It was only much later that this widely held conviction was revealed to be in error.

What do we honestly know as we look at the body of material from our prehistoric past? We know that a site, or an artifact, was unearthed in a specific location. These particulars are facts. In the same breath, many assumptions are made regarding their use, utility, meaning, and role in society.

Dolmen, according to academics, are ancient burial sites. Nevertheless, the reality is no one knows who, why or when dolmen were constructed. There is no direct evidence providing us with an answer. Human remains and artifacts, at some locations, have been found and dated. These finds do not

Chapter 14: More Questions Than Answers

offer definitive proof of when the original structure was erected. It also does not provide insights into its use. Scholars, instead of stating, we think dolmen were burial sites, put out their beliefs and suppositions as unquestionable facts. Their baseless claims are often accepted by an entire generation when the reality is their declarations may be correct or may be just a figment of *their wild imagination*.

Figure 89 - Recently discovered cup depicting a representation of the *God of the Golden Arches*. Image courtesy of Padeia

A pot is found in an ancient ruin, the fragment of a figurine is unearthed. The party line often describes the item as being used for *ritualistic purposes*. Did the archeologist attend the ritual in which it was used? Is there a video, a book or even a stone tablet describing its use? Imagine it is 5000, 10,000 or 50,000 years in the future and society loses its ability to interpret texts from this period. Then one day a future archeologist, digging in a trash heap somewhere outside St. Louis uncovers a plastic McDonald's cup and then another (Fig. 89). Would his assumption that these cups had some implicit value to us be true? If he contends that we worshiped not only the *God of the Golden Arches* but a fertility goddess we in the 21st century call *Wendy*, would his speculation be correct? The answer would be a resounding NO!

We can only hypothesize when talking about our remote past. We can take the evidence in hand and with a bit of interpretation derive a working theory as to what is going on. It is the **interpretation** of the data that can make all of the difference in the world. One thing you may have noticed, as you have read this text so far, are the vast changes in positions and beliefs scientists make as new and exciting discoveries are brought forward. Concepts, which were at one time held as factual and accurate representations of the topic at hand, are merely abandoned when a bit of fresh evidence or a newfangled interpretation comes to the forefront.

Huge assertions are often made based upon a small bit of pottery, an isolated tooth, a skull fragment or even a recovered animal bone. What they fail to understand is that the foundation of who we are, unlike stones and bones, leaves no record. Culture, that complex part of us which includes our beliefs, values, norms, ideals, laws, and customs may linger on in the cultural memory of a group, but they do not leave traces. They exist in our hearts and minds, in our history and cannot be dug up by archaeologists in their excavations. Thus, it is not considered, by the same explorers into the past, scientific nor evidence. The broken pot, the rock-hewn structure, the ancient burial, the ceremonial mask were all fashioned to satisfy the needs of a group's culture and could only be shaped through the use of cultural knowledge. It is a heritage of skills, stories, songs, ceremonies, and rituals that have been transmitted from one generation to another. Without it, who would we be?

Researchers have come to recognize that all of humanity, regardless of location, share a variety of behaviors which include:

- Verbal communication, including rules of grammar and sentence construction.
- The classification of individuals based on age, gender, marital and kinship relationships.
- The rearing of children in a family setting.
- The division of labor according to sex.
- The concept of privacy.
- Rules of sexual behavior.
- Guidelines that identify good and bad behavior.
- Body ornamentation.
- Joking and playing games.
- Art and artistic expression.
- The establishment of leadership roles within a community.

Chapter 14: More Questions Than Answers

Some anthropologists contend as we have already discussed that these and other cultural traits are biologically inherited. They also suggest that the parallel behaviors found around the world developed independently. They go on to explain, while all nations have these and possibly many other universal traits, each culture develops their own specific ways of carrying out and expressing their particular traditions.

Our list, as you can see, extends far beyond those established by mainstream science. And while some of the traditions we explored do not appear in every culture, it is impossible to assume that at some time or another they did not. Just because there is not any tangible, hard evidence to prove it one way or the other does not mean it did not exist.

What we do know and can provide a reasonable conclusion to is that when you place world cultures side by side, the chances the founding principles they display would follow such a clear and consistent pattern are astronomical and statistically improbable. The unparalleled similarities found in these cultural traits do not suggest that they were invented independently but lend credence to the theory that they originated from a single source. It points to the fact that we were at one time all one cultural group or learned from the same teacher. Then, over time and location, subcultures formed leaving us with the diversity we see today.

It must be restated, as we delve into some uncharted territory, that the date applied to a bone or a piece of pottery does not indicate the origin of a tradition. It does not establish a conclusive date as to when a behavior began. It lets us know that a procedure was used at the time, yet the method may have been in its infancy when the object was created or may have been in use for an extended period, a time unknown to us. Likewise, items made of perishable materials; skin, straw, flowers, leaves, wood, and bone rarely leave traces behind. Therefore, traditions such as tattooing, mask making, body painting and even circumcision, may have a history far older than can be seen in the archeological record.

With these challenges in hand, we will begin the arduous task of trying to make sense of a timeline associated with the education and development of humanity. The timeline is based on what has been found in the archeological record as well as other supporting evidence we have uncovered. As we move forward, you will quickly realize that this is not what you have been taught in school.

A Journey Through Time

Earlier, we learned from the mythic record that the gods are sighted as being the teachers of humanity. From fire to metallurgy, they are the ones credited with our training. We also discussed how one record survived that described the timing of this education. It came from the Babylonian priest Berosus who described the half man/half fish creatures, the Oannes, who emerged from the Erythraean Sea six times over the course of our history. They are credited with instructing humanity in the arts and sciences and providing us with a moral code to live by.

Could the claims of Berosus be true? Could the gods (the Oannes) have appeared here on Earth, not just once but over vast periods of time? If one of the earliest gifts of the gods were fire, then it would only make sense that the skills associated with metallurgy and agriculture would have come much later in our history. Can we track the appearance of the gods here on Earth by the sudden emergence of new genetic traits, lines of thoughts or advancing technologies?

We will be starting our endeavor identifying the timing of our educational history with one of the most consistent global myth we find on the planet. It is the story commonly associated with the biblical character Noah and the flood ascribed to him. Without recounting the story narrative, we will instead be focusing on when this tragic event occurred. (ET Chronicles – The Flood)

Chapter 14: More Questions Than Answers

Putting the flood into historical perspective is challenging at best. It has been dated to 2400 BC, 6000 BC, and most recently to around 11,500 BC. Sadly, physical evidence to support a global flood and its associated narrative does not exist regardless of the period selected. If the flood occurred on or around any of these dates, they do not account for how parallel flood narratives are found in the Americas and on the Australian continent. These remote locations were inhabited long before any of these proposed dates.

You find a different potential date for the flood when you evaluate the few clues that myth records. These ancient narratives place the flood to a period of between 30–40,000 years ago. In my attempt to close in on the real date of the flood, a startling pattern emerged. It appeared as I was researching my book ET Chronicles. (ET Chronicles - The Flood)

Starting at around 40,000 years ago and moving forward, we find three major radar-like blips on the currently accepted timeline. At about 40,000 years ago we experienced considerable strides in culture and technology. Call the *creative explosion* this period gave rise to the first intricate cave painting, figurative art and early fired pottery. Twisted and dyed flax fibers have been found which suggests the early stages of textile production. (Remember the myth that details how humanity learned to grow flax and weave it?) We began collecting and grinding wild grains to make flatbread. It was also during this time that the first genetic miracle in the wheat family occurred where wild einkorn wheat mixed with goat grass to produce emmer wheat. This explosion in art and technology started off strong and began to dwindle. In total, this rash of new technology and innovation lasted for over 10,000 years and then for some unknown reason everything seemed to quiet down. No significant advancements took place for thousands of years.

The domestication of plants and animals was the next major spur in technological innovation to appear. The earliest indication of the cultivation of domestic, versus wild wheat, appears about 10,000 BC. Evidence suggests that these farmers, within only two to three centuries, were able to figure out how to engineer and domesticate this finicky grain. This period is also when we find the second miraculous genetic change to the structure of wheat.

One would logically assume that the expertise required to domesticate plants would have originated in one area and then would have radiated out from this location. This movement of technological knowledge is not what we find. Not long after wheat was domesticated in the Fertile Crescent, early forms of domestic rice suddenly appeared in Asia, while Indian corn made its debut in the Americas. Domesticated animals saw a similar, quick and widespread rise with some of the first domesticated aminals appearing as early as 8500 BC. This trend in animal husbandry popped up around the globe and progressed at a rapid pace until about 2500 BC where it abruptly stopped. The total number of animals that have been domesticated in the 5000 years since, in spite of our advancing technology, is ***zero***!

This period also saw the advent of many forms of body modification, including the elongation of skulls, trepanation, and dental modifications. What occurred to foster these painful procedures is a mystery. Proof of the worldwide use of entheogen appears, although their consumption may have begun earlier. And then again, like in the earlier stage, all is quiet, and significant advances are nil.

Humanity took another massive stride about 3500 BC with the sudden appearance of *civilization* in Sumner. Technological advances included the development of writing, astrology, astronomy, monumental architecture, metallurgy, the wheel and a codified set of laws. After this spurt in technological growth, advancements slow down once more and practically stop again for thousands of years. The appearance of a system of writing, however, allowed us to document our lives and preserve at least some of our history. So while we may not know the whole truth, from this point forward, we do possess at least some clues to our past.

Can we attribute these emerging patterns of improvements in the human experience to the visitations of

Chapter 14: More Questions Than Answers

the gods and the education they provided us? If that is the case, can we, using the same parameters, look further back in time and perceive when the gods may have interacted with humanity before the flood?

If we look at the development of our paleolithic ancestors, remarkably, a similar pattern of episodic growth with great intervals of stalled advancements quickly emerges. The first significant blip in our timeline occurs around 4 million years ago with the introduction of our bipedal ancestor *Australopithecus* and the appearance of crafted stone tools.

The evolution of humanity took on an accelerated pace with the rise of *Homo erectus*. In addition to considerable physiological changes, they demonstrated a developing level of cognitive understanding. They showed early signs of culture and had learned to work with and control our first gift from the gods, fire. The carved shell, from Java, Indonesia, testifies to their developing abilities. The simple inscribed lines on the shells suggest that the geometric motif had an implied or intrinsic meaning. It is during this window that *Homo Naladi* performed intention burials. Evidence of early ochre use can also be found. Were our *Homo erectus* ancestors already developing traditions such as ritual sacrifices and the sacred caribberie? (ET Chronicles – The Age of Man)

We find interesting insights into this query when we explore Hindu cosmology. By 869,100 years ago, according to Hindu tradition, we had left the *Treta Yuga* and moved into the *Dwapara Yuga*. Rama, the hero of the *Ramayana*, as you may recall, lived during the Treta Yuga. Each epoch or era within this four-age cyclical system is associated with specific characteristics in human consciousness. Starting at its highest point, in a *Golden Age of Enlightenment*, the *Satya Yuga*, human consciousness gradually declines until it reaches a dark age of evil and ignorance, the *Kali Yuga*. From this low point, texts indicate that consciousness will begin to shift back upward until it returns to a Golden Age again. (ET Chronicles - Cycles of Time)

The Dwapara Yuga is believed to be an age in which humanity's connection to the unseen world starts to wane. It is

Stepping Out of Eden

associated with a decline in righteousness, morality, and virtue. People during this time became more competitive, zealous, deceitful and pleasure-seeking. As a whole, our intellect dwindles causing a gradual loss of awareness to the higher laws of energy and the subtle world. Our focus becomes more allied with the world of matter. This increased connection to the material world reduced our ability to unite with the divine and be part of the natural world. Was our developing technology a byproduct of entering into the Dwapara Yuga?

Additionally, the Dwapara Yuga, according to these same texts, saw the commencement of *varnas* or social classes. The initiation of varnas divided society into four groups – a caste system. This caste system dictated the type of occupations a person could pursue and the social interactions that he or she may have. It was represented by the *Brahmin* or priestly class, the *Kshatriyas*, the class of rulers and warriors, the *Vaishyas*, which included landowners and merchants and the *Shudra*, who involved themselves in highly physical labor (Fig. 90).

Figure 90 - The 4 Varnas of the Indian caste system.

Of interest to our discussion is the Brahmin varna. Contemplation, meditation, charity and teaching activities filled their lives. They performed these duties in order to attain celestial bliss and the grace of the divine. They were the protectors of sacred learning across generations and the repository of sacrosanct knowledge.

Were rituals created to enable the Brahmin, the medicine men, shamans and early priests the means to continue communicating with the gods? Were body modification, such as circumcision, required of these holy men to identify their role and position in society? Equally, was a god-king and laws, such as marriage, put in place to control and monitor the spread of the upgraded *Homo erectus* genetic code? Did a system of taboos help these early leaders manage the increasing degradation of society?

And although our earliest suggestive evidence of circumcision does not appear until about 30,000 years ago, it is believed that this body modification pre-dates recorded history and may have existed before the movement of anatomically modern man around the globe. Günter Wagner, in his book *The Bantu of North Kavirondo* suggests, *"The distribution of circumcision and initiation rites throughout Africa, and the frequent resemblance between details of ceremonial procedure in areas thousands of miles apart, indicate that the circumcision ritual has an old tradition behind it and in its present form is the result of a long process of development."* Is it possible that this painful surgical procedure in point of fact began with our *Homo erectus* ancestors?

Our next blip appears around 80,000-00 years ago, when humanity took another noteworthy cognitive shift. Here we find evidence of the intentional burial of *Homo neanderthalensis* and *Homo sapiens*. Bodies unearthed have been discovered lying on their side in a flexed position, covered with ochre and interred with grave goods. Tied to this dynamic time of innovation, is the appearance of our first piece of *art*, the carved piece of ochre found at Blombos Cave (Fig. 33), the world's first jewelry, the pierced shell beads and the inscribed ostrich eggshells. The use of herbs and herbal medicine may have found its advent during this time of immense change and innovation.

Data also indicates that at this point in human history populations sharply decreased, which created a bottleneck in human evolution. Estimates suggest that the number of people living during this time was reduced to between 3000 and 10,000 individuals. This conclusion was reached based on genetic evidence, which indicates that humans today descended from a relatively small population of breeding pairs.

For years, this genetic bottleneck has been linked to the eruption of Mount Toba, a super volcano on the island of Sumatra. Mount Toba had erupted many times in the past but the explosion that occurred about 74,000 years ago was believed to have cut down a significant portion of the Earth's population. The Mount Toba eruption, when put into perspective, was more than 5000 times larger than the 1980's eruption of Mount St Helens in Washington State.

Recent discoveries, however, indicate that the Mount Toba eruption may not have decimated human populations as was once thought. According to the traditional view of human development and their migration patterns, modern humans did not arrive in Asia until about 60,000 years ago. That date is 14,000 years after the Mount Toba eruption. Finds unearthed in southern India are casting doubt on this long-held belief.

Artifacts found in a valley in southern India indicate that anatomically modern man was living in the region both before and after the blast. These suppositions are based on stone tools that were found in sediment just below the ash layer as well as just above it. Researchers initially thought that the stone tools recovered were the work of an earlier human species. Recently, archaeologists discovered a new stone-tool culture that extended from 74,000 years until 7,000 years ago. The tools they crafted were all manufactured in a similar style. They realized that the technology they used had not changed over this long span and concluded that modern humans must have created them all. The inescapable implication of this find is that people were living near Mount Toba both before and after the volcano blew and survived this super-eruption.

If the Toba explosion did not produce a genetic bottleneck as researchers have suggested, then what kind of catastrophe was large enough to have done the job? A tsunami perhaps?

The eruption of the volcano on the island of Santorini in the Aegean Sea and the subsequent massive waves that shot across the Mediterranean Sea has long been blamed for the destruction of the entire Minoan civilization. The 1815 eruption of Mount Tambora, on Sumbawa Island, Indonesia,

Chapter 14: More Questions Than Answers

was the first massive eruption recorded in modern times. Indonesia's islands, after the blast, were struck by tsunami waves reaching up to 13 ft (4 meters) in height. One of the largest and most destructive tsunamis ever recorded occurred after the explosion of the volcano on Krakatoa (Krakatau), in Indonesia on August 26, 1883. This blast generated waves that reached 135 feet (41 meters) in height.

Did a massive tsunami, triggered by the eruption of Mount Toba, devastate humanity? Could the dates provided for the flood, whether biblical, via ancient texts or modern researchers all be wrong? Evidence does seem to support this notion.

If mankind were reduced to just a few remaining individuals, as the flood narrative suggests, one **would** expect to see a genetic bottleneck in human evolution. Scientifically speaking it accounts for the discontinuities observed in our genetic lineage. It explains the common characteristics, traits, behaviors, and customs found around the world. It explicates the universalities found in myth. It also details why there is not any evidence of a worldwide flood, especially in the last 40,000 years. Did the cultural and behavioral traits of one of the surviving group, which includes their story of devastation and destruction, spread across the landscape?

Researchers, such as Michael Witzel, a Professor of Sanskrit at Harvard University, support this line of thought. In his book, *The Origins of the World's Mythologies*, Witzel suggests that the flood occurred at least 100,000 years ago. This date, he contends precedes the movement of modern man out of Africa. Based on the consistency found in world myth, he believes that the events that took place were part of a single group's history. As this cultural group moved across Eurasia and into Australia and the Americas, their rituals, traditions and epic narratives went along with them. His assertions deserve merit when looking at the character of our ancient legends and the commonalities found in various cultures.

In any case, advancements seem to settle down until about 40,000 years ago. According to the First People of Australia, after the flood, the *Alcheringa*, the Dreamtime, the time of the gods ended as well.

The Million-Dollar Question

This is where we get to the million-dollar question. Why did a group of gods come to the Earth in the first place? Why did they create us, educate us? Unfortunately, mythology tends to be very quiet on the why side of things. Contemporary science does not acknowledge or address this potential issue.

In his book series *The 12th Planet*, authors such as Zecharia Sitchin, propose that humanity (*Homo sapiens*) were created as primitive laborers to replace a group of overworked rank-and-file *Anunnaki* who had rebelled. The Anunnaki, based upon his interpretation of ancient Sumerian texts, are a band of space travelers who came to the Earth from their homeworld *Nibiru*. They sought out the Earth because of it vast gold resources.

Gold mining activities on the Earth, according to Sitchen, commenced about 450,000 years ago. The recovered ore was transported back to their homeworld and was used to repair its failing atmosphere. Genetic engineering, the mixing of the genes of the planets erect primates with that of the Anunnaki, began about 200,000 years ago. This newly created hybrid race then took on the job of extracting gold from the depths of the Earth. *"They wanted to create primitive workers from the Homo erectus and give him the genes to allow him to think and use tools."* Zecharia Sitchin claims.

In a similar vein to Sitchen's premise, author Michael Tellinger in his book, *Slave Species Of The Gods*, takes this notion one step further. He proposes that humanity was created as a slave race to serve the needs of the gods. He goes on to identify a complex of sophisticated ruins in South Africa, complete with thousands of gold mines, whose operations were wiped out by the flood. He contends that these acts began our global tradition of gold obsession, slavery, and god as a dominating master.

Scary as this may be to think about, were we actually their slaves? Does myth support any of these claims?

Chapter 14: More Questions Than Answers

Greek and Hindu cosmology inform us that a race of giants lived on the Earth before the advent of humanity. In the Greek world, the giants were created from the blood of the castrated god Uranus. These *Earth-born* creatures worked for many years on massive building projects for the gods. They believed, over time, they were above the tasks assigned to them. They were after all *"the sons and daughters of the gods."* War broke out between the giants and the gods with the gods winning the rebellion. It was decided, once the hostilities concluded, that the gods would create a new race of workers to perform their labors - mankind. (ET Chronicles – The Rebellion)

From the Sumerian *Atra-hasis Epic*, we find a similar story. In it, a group of lesser gods called the *Igigi* worked for years as laborers. Eventually, they revolted. It was their revolution that caused the creation of humankind. Another potential reference to the exploits of early man comes from the Sumerian tale of *Enki and Ninmah*, where the god Enki is quoted as saying, *"My mother, the creature you planned will really come into existence. Impose on him the work of carrying baskets."*

There are some indications in Sumerian texts that our ancestors may have lived and worked as miners digging up lapis lazuli, precious metals, and gemstones or as farmers in fields. In these texts, little mention of gold is made, and references to gold mining are never revealed. If the Anunnaki's primary intention were to recover gold, then one would think that it would be a common theme running through their narratives. It is not. (ET Chronicles – The Fight For Immortality)

An analogous concept is portrayed in the Mayan Popol Vuh, where the gods created animals to serve them by carrying heavy burdens. The gods wanted to be venerated and worshiped, but the animals lacked this capability. It was decided to create a new creature to fill this role; thus humanity was formed. Our final reference comes from the *Ramayana*, where the Vanara, the ape-men, were created to help Rama secure a victory against Ravana, the Demon God of Lanka.

If we were slaves created by the gods, it is evident that we have not performed this kind of heavy labor on their behalf for millennia. If we had, stories of our indentured servitude would appear somewhere in our mythic history. One would think a prayer to the gods asking for their intervention would have been written, a ritual created or some evidence of our hard work would exist, yet these acts are not documented on a clay tablet, a bit of papyrus, wood or animal skins. In fact, other than the few vague allusion to it, no such texts exist.

It does seem more likely, based upon humanities relationship with the gods, that we were created not as a slave race, but as a domesticated species, perhaps an animal of labor akin to a horse or camel. The gods, instead of treating us insensitively and cruelly, cared for us in much the same way we love and care for our pets. In a way, we may liken our treatment to the training received by sign-language chimpanzees such as Washoe. (ET Chronicles – Unnatural Selection)

Washoe was raised like a child by her handlers Allen and Beatrix Gardner. She frequently wore clothes and sat with them to eat at the dinner table. She had access to clothing, combs, toys, books, and a toothbrush and like a human child had a routine of chores to perform. Unfortunately, studies such as the one done with Washoe are often ended as the apes grow into adulthood. We will never know if the education provided to these apes would be passed down, like the sweet potato washing behavior of the macaque monkeys, to future generations.

Another theory, that details why we were created, comes from individuals such as David Icke. In his book *The Biggest Secret*, for example, he claims that the Anunnaki are in fact a reptilian race from the Draco constellation. These extraterrestrial reptilians lived in enormous catacombs, caverns, and tunnels below the surface of the Earth. According to Icke, the Anunnaki bred with humans to produce a human-reptoid race between 200,000 and 300,000 years ago. A second and third breeding program began later and are dated to about 30,000 and 7000 years ago respectfully. He contends

Chapter 14: More Questions Than Answers

that the creatures born in the last breeding program, the *Babylonian Brotherhood*, also known as the *Illuminati*, are the ones who are in control of the world today.

Icke further claims that the reptilians bred with the tall, blonde-haired alien race known as the Nordics. It was through this genetic mixing that character traits including cold-bloodedness, obsession with ritual, desire for top-down leadership and a tendency toward fascism emerged. He goes on to suggest that we were not created as a slave race, but instead as a food source for the reptilians. They would not eat us physically, like a well-cooked meal. Instead, they would feed off of our emotional energy.

As human beings, we each vibrate, depending on our mood, at a specific frequency. When we feel connected, inspired or enthusiastic, we emanate a high-energy vibration. When we are sad, afraid, stressed, depressed, anxious, angry or frustrated, the vibration we emit is low. Authors, such as Icke, believe that the reptilians consume these low energy vibrations. It can be likened to the power human life supplied the machines in the movie *The Matrix*. Knowledge, he suggests, even some of the earliest pieces of technology the gods gave us started us down the long road to providing sustenance to the Reptilians.

Figure 91 - Adam & Eve as they eat from the Tree of Knowledge.

Myth does support many of the concepts put forth by Icke and other researchers from his camp. The Book of Genesis, for example, recounts how a wise serpent revealed to Adam and Eve forbidden knowledge (Fig. 91). *"For God knows that when you eat from it your eyes will be opened, and you will be like God, knowing good and evil."* This act, the act of educating humanity, went against the will of God and everyone, Adam, Eve and the serpent were punished. The god who provided humanity fire, one of the first pieces of technology obtained by humanity, also went against the will of the gods and is punished for his act. The myriad of gods associated with these dastardly deeds are consistently described in a negative light.

This is where we get into the rub. This same character, in many cultures, is also associated with the creation (genetic engineering) of humanity. As a benefactor of mankind, he or his emissaries provided humankind knowledge and wisdom. He is the one credited with warning individuals, such as Noah, about the impending flood. In his role as an advocate for humanity, he often finds himself in an uncomfortable position, as being an adversary to the gods.

Some people point to these instances as proof that this god was benevolent and wanted good things for humanity. Others suggest that he only taught humanity precisely what he wanted us to know and nothing more. The emphasis of his role changing from a humanitarian mission performed by a beneficial god to one where we are being manipulated, with the gods ultimately benefiting from the outcome. Were we provided with an education (as well as genetic enhancements) to ensure our independence or was something more sinister at work? Dinner perhaps?

This claim, however, brings up a variety of interesting points. Why all of the cloak and dagger operations if this is the case? If the reptilians have been on Earth for hundreds of thousands of years, why give us any control in the first place? With their advanced technology, they could have maintained their role as gods and no one would be the wiser.

And why bother giving humanity intelligence? Why teach us to how to control fire, plant crops, build monumental structures and track the stars? By providing humanity with the rules to live by, was it their goal to turn us into an increasingly passive species? These changes to our culture did set us on the course of living and thriving in more densely populated urban settings. The introduction of agriculture accelerated this. It spurred on population growth and the tensions associated with large groups of people living in a confined environment. Was it the reptilian's objective to corral us up into self-made pens so they can more easily feed upon us? The answer is still out on that one.

Who Are We?

Did we evolve from the world's great apes and then somehow developed an intellect, consciousness, and self-awareness as evolutionists contend or were we created, molded, and educated by the gods as myth portrays? Likewise, did our traditions, laws, and customs come from a universal unconscious conviction that manifested themselves as a consistent pattern of social evolution or were these traits impressed upon us by a higher source? Researchers to this day still cannot explain how or why so many things in our world, including our culture, seem so consistent and deliberate.

Taken to its core, who would we be without the education and edicts provided for us by the gods? If the gods had not appointed these things, would they exist at all? Was it our inherent nature, our destiny, to leave the jungles, forests, and savannas and transform ourselves or were we living in a virtual paradise, that is, until we ate of the forbidden fruit? What was the cost? Expulsion from a world of sentient bliss?

In an episode of *Star Trek: The Next Generation* entitled *Who Watches The Watchers*, the USS Enterprise is called to help a group of anthropologists who were studying a proto-Vulcan culture. Through a series of inopportune events, a local man and his daughter see members of the anthropological team and the Enterprise's crew. Shocked by what he sees, the man falls. It is decided to care for his injury onboard the

Enterprise. His new surroundings are a magnificent place filled with wonders. At one point in the episode, the man observes Captain Picard giving orders to his crew and concludes that Captain Picard is a god.

Is this what happened to us? Have we interacted with an advanced race and in our ignorance elevated them to godhood? Were we at one time a grand science experiment?

If, as this treatise suggests, we were educated and conditioned by the gods, how much programming have we encountered? Have we been manipulated our whole lives? If this is the case, our indoctrination started as soon as we exited the womb and will continue until we take our last breath.

Today, many people speak about our unalienable rights and our ability to express free will. Free will is the facility to choose between different possible courses of action unimpeded. Do we actually have control over our thoughts and actions? If you think about it, much of what we know, much of what we hold true is just a repetition of what we have learned, right, wrong or indifferent. Case and point: Who discovered America? Regardless of your final answer, everyone's initial kneejerk internalized first response to this question is always Christopher Columbus (Fig. 92). Jerry A. Coyne, a Professor of Ecology and Evolution at The University of Chicago claims *"Free will is an illusion so convincing that people simply refuse to believe that we don't have it."*

Figure 92 - Portrait of Christopher Columbus.

Chapter 14: More Questions Than Answers

Animals, excluding those that have been domesticated (educated), do not live by a glaring set of rules, regulations, and traditions that control or limit their behavior. They do not decree what is acceptable versus not. It is interesting because even with all of our laws, morals and social mores, our ability to live by these prescribed codes has seemingly failed. Many do not think twice about lying, cheating, stealing or worse.

Then what is our true nature? Today, the focus of human attention is on the material world, the world we experience with our five senses. We are taught that things outside of what we can see, smell, hear, taste or touch do not exist. Anyone who believes there is more to this world or sense things that fall outside of this limited vantage point are looked down upon, ridiculed, condemned or identified as being broken or wrong. It was vastly different in antiquity. The world was seen as living and breathing, a place filled with energy and spirits. Our appreciation of this non-material universe and the interconnectedness of all things has for the most part been lost.

It is certain that our ancestors, as we see in modern indigenous cultures, had a far more expanded awareness and connection to the world around them. Native American myth, for example, informs us that at one time, people could talk to the animals. They worked and played together in peace and harmony. Did our education create a rift in our ability to interact with the world in the way we had before? Returning to our earlier discussion on our formative training and the *Epic of Gilgamesh* in particular, we know that once Gilgamesh's friend Enkidu learned the ways of man, the animals, who had been his family in the past, distanced themselves from him.

> *But when he turned his attention to his animals,*
> *the gazelles saw Enkidu and darted off,*
> *the wild animals distanced themselves from his body.*
>
> – The Epic of Gilgamesh, Tablet I

Figure 93 - Was God repackaged?

Chapter 14: More Questions Than Answers

Is this connection to the seen and unseen world our natural state of being? Did the very act that instigated the development of humanity as we know it, create a schism between the natural world and us? Most of us have lost our connection to every other living thing on the planet. We envision ourselves as being separate and apart from it. Sadly, in the west, we have developed a belief that we have a God-given right to dominate everything and everyone. Let the plants and animals of the Earth be damned. Instead of being part of nature, we have isolated ourselves from it. But why? Wouldn't it be *more human* to be in harmony with the world around us?

Then there are the gods such as Zeus, Enki, Thor, Indra, and Quetzalcoatl. What happened to them? Do they miss us? Perhaps we are still idolizing the same pantheon of gods except repackaged and renamed (Fig. 93). (ET Chronicles – A God By Any Other Name)

One thing does seem clear when talking about the gods is that in cultures around the world stories exist that tell us that they will be coming back. The Inca identified the god Viracocha as the one who would return, where the Aztec state Quetzalcoatl will reappear. Christians believe Jesus will make an appearance after the rapture and end of days. But then again, is our recollection of a returning god true or is it something we conjured up to give us hope in trying times. If as mythology suggests they do return, will they upgrade our hardware or provide us with more advanced knowledge and technology as they had in the past?

One question many ask is *"did they ever leave at all"*? The teachers of humanity seemed to have disappeared for vast periods of time as we learned with the half man/half fish, the Oannas. Where were they during these intervening periods? Did they return to their heavenly abode, their home planet or did they travel to some undisclosed remote location? Could their declaration of a return be more congruent with a friend that lives in a distant town or city? We might not be able to visit daily or even weekly, but at the conclusion of our time together, a promise is made to come back to visit. Is this scenario a possibility with the gods?

If the gods did not leave, where have they been all of this time?

Today, instead of talking about gods soaring through the sky on fiery chariots, we speak of UFO's, strange aerial phenomena and alien visitation. Are these beings related to the gods of old? Have we come to recognize them in their correct form, not as omnipotent beings but as otherworldly visitors with advanced technology? If that is the case, then maybe they have never left at all. Perhaps they are still, up there, beyond the clouds watching over us.

About Rita Louise, PhD

Bestselling author Dr. Rita Louise is the founder of the Institute of Applied Energetics and the host of Just Energy Radio. She is a Naturopathic Physician and a 20-year veteran in the Human Potential Field. Her unique gift as a medical intuitive and clairvoyant illuminates and enlivens her work. She is the author of the books *ET Chronicles: What Myth And Legend Have To Say About Human Origin*, *Avoiding The Cosmic 2X4*, *Dark Angels: An Insider's Guide To Ghosts, Spirits & Attached Entities* and *The Power Within*.

She is also the producer of a number of feature length as well as video shorts. Their titles include: *iKon: Deconstructing The Archetypes Of The Ancients*, *Holy Deception*, *Ancient Aliens, Genetic Engineering & The Rise Of Civilization*, *The Truth About The Nephilim Giants*, *Deceit, Lies & Deception: The Reptilian Agenda*, *Paranormal Phenomena: Attached Entities – The Bad Kids Of The Spirit World*, *Ghosts, Gods & Myth*, *The Secret To The Law Of Attraction* and *Reincarnation: Have We Been Here Before*?

Dr. Louise credits early childhood influences for the direction her life would take. By the age of 8, she developed a deep interest in ancient traditions, culture, archaeology and human origins. As time went on, she began searching for spiritual self-discovery pursuing topics including health and wellness, philosophy and the esoteric arts and sciences. Dr. Louise graduated San Jose State University with a degree in Industrial Design and worked as an electro-mechanical designer and Engineering Services Manager in the military industrial complex. She is a graduate of the Berkeley Psychic Institute where she studied meditation, energy medicine, and learned how to perform clairvoyant readings. After establishing a private practice, Dr. Louise returned to school full time, earning a degree as a Naturopath and then a Ph.D. in Natural Health Counseling.

A frequent consultant to the media, Dr. Louise has appeared on television and film and has mystified listeners during her countless radio interviews. Dr. Louise has appeared as a keynote speaker at hundreds of events around the country where she has spoken on topics such as ancient mysteries, mythology, ancient aliens, intuition, ghosts and the paranormal. Her countless writings have appeared in books, magazines and newsletters around the world.

Her webpage is SoulHealer.com.

The E.T. Chronicles: What Myths and Legends Tell Us About Human Origins

Rita Louise, PhD

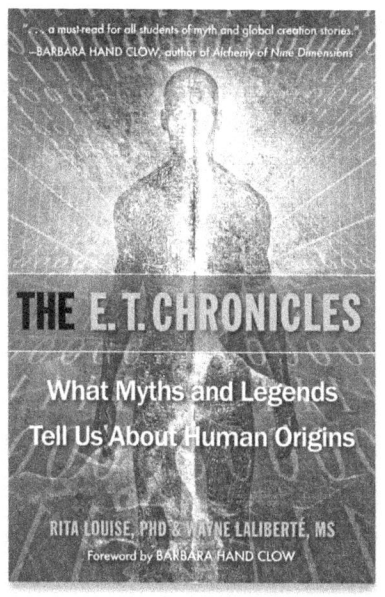

The E.T. Chronicles is a startling and comprehensive examination of ancient myths and legends that describe extraterrestrial visitors and their encounters with humanity since the dawn of time. Organized into a chronology that starts with "*in the beginning*" and ends with the advent of civilization, it brings together myths from many cultures (including the Sumerians, the Greek, the Maya and the Aborigines of Australia) and explores them in the context of current scientific discoveries.

The result is a mind-blowing re-visioning of human origins through close reading of ancient texts relating to: creation, gods and goddesses, heaven, the gods and their toys (space ships or chariots?), the quest for immortality

Could it be that those ancient stories of the gods were more than just the product of someone's fanciful imagination? Is it possible that the writers, chroniclers, and scribes of our distant past actually record an accurate view of our origin? Could it be that we are really children of the stars?

> "*Absolutely fascinating and a must read for anyone interested in the 'extraterrestrial question' of the origins of humanity.*"
> Robert M. Schoch, Ph.D.

Dark Angels: An Insider's Guide To Ghosts, Spirits & Attached Entities

Rita Louise, PhD

When talking about beings without bodies; angels, ascended masters and spirit guides aren't the only kids on the block. Dark Angels talks about the bad kids in town. Who are these bad kids? As a child, you might have met one at night...under your bed, in your closet or down a dark hallway. What are we talking about? We are talking about ghosts, spirits and attached entities.

Dark Angels is an exciting exploration into the darker side of the spirit world. This isn't a dull dissertation about ghosts. It takes a fun and candid approach to addressing ghosts, attached entities and demons. Dark Angels is filled with revealing information about these "*dark forces*" and how they can influence our lives.

Written in a straightforward, easy to read manner, the technical content as well as the stories shared are infused with Dr. Louise's own wit, candor and sassy style.

Dr. Rita Louise has done it again with her new book Dark Angels!
Wayne L. – Dallas, TX

Films by Rita Louise, PhD

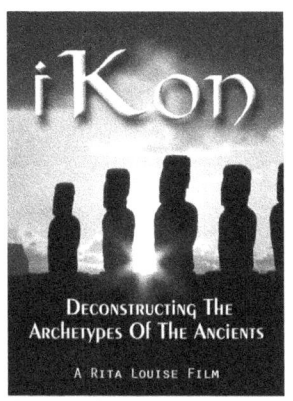

iKon: Deconstructing the Archetypes of the Ancients

Rita Louise, PhD

iKon: Deconstructing The Archetypes of the Ancients challenges you to open your mind to a completely new way of thinking of our past, a past that is being hidden from us, yet is right in front of our very eyes. Are you ready to step outside the box of conventional thought?

Holy Deception

Rita Louise, PhD

What do you believe about God? Holy Deception challenges you to reexamine your notion of God while looking at what other cultures, both past and present have to say. Is our current perception of God actually a flight of fantasy? Could we have been deceived and our notion of a kind and benevolent omnipotent creator god be fallacious? Dr. Rita Louise's new film is a mix of Ancient Aliens VS. the Bible!

Available on Amazon.com

www.ingramcontent.com/pod-product-compliance
Lightning Source LLC
Chambersburg PA
CBHW061255110426
42742CB00012BA/1923